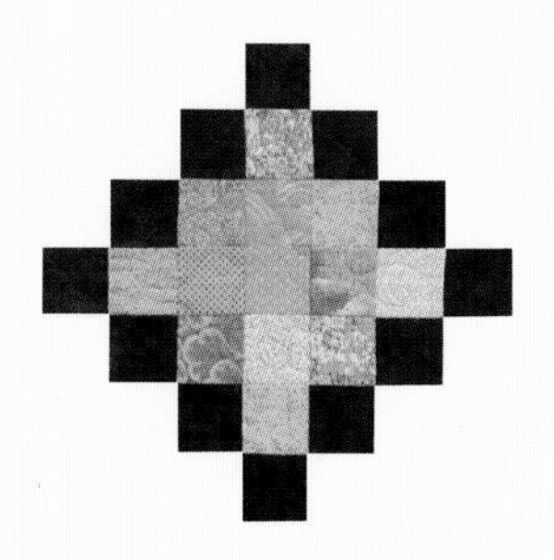

S is for SCRAPS

18 great quilts

Gayle Bong

Credits

President & CEO: Tom Wierzbicki

Editor in Chief: Mary V. Green

Managing Editor: Tina Cook

Developmental Editor: Karen Costello Soltys

Technical Editor: Laurie Baker

Copy Editor: Marcy Heffernan

Design Director: Stan Green

Production Manager: Regina Girard

Illustrator: Adrienne Smitke

Cover & Text Designer: Shelly Garrison

Photographer: Brent Kane

Mission Statement

Dedicated to providing quality products and service to inspire creativity.

S is for Scraps: 18 Great Quilts

That Patchwork Place® is an imprint of Martingale & Company®.

Martingale & Company
19021 120th Ave. NE, Suite 102
Bothell, WA 98011 USA
www.martingale-pub.com

Printed in China
15 14 13 12 11 10 8 7 6 5 4 3 2 1

Library of Congress Cataloging-in-Publication Data is available upon request.

ISBN: 978-1-56477-993-9

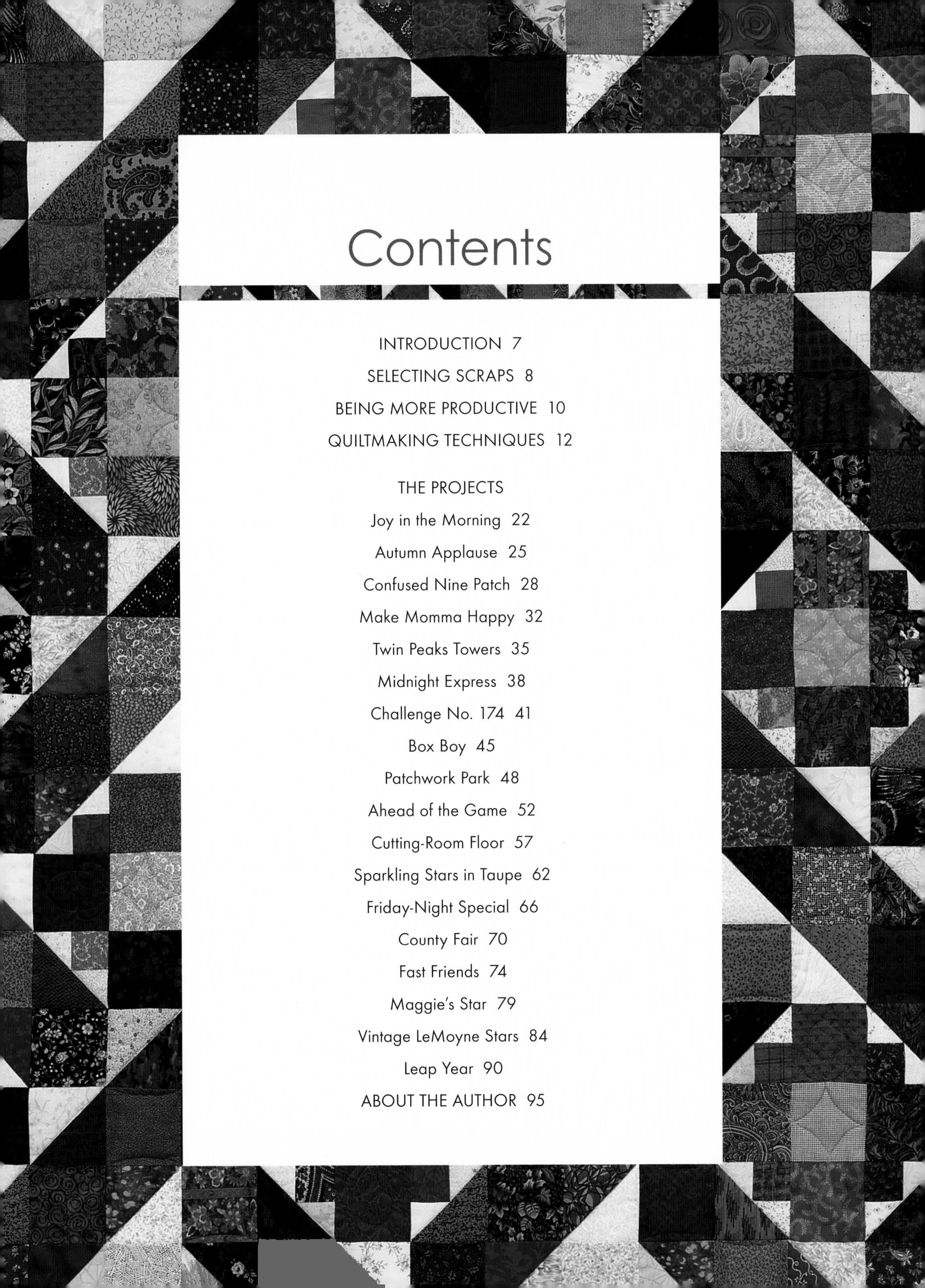

Contents

INTRODUCTION 7

SELECTING SCRAPS 8

BEING MORE PRODUCTIVE 10

QUILTMAKING TECHNIQUES 12

THE PROJECTS

Joy in the Morning 22

Autumn Applause 25

Confused Nine Patch 28

Make Momma Happy 32

Twin Peaks Towers 35

Midnight Express 38

Challenge No. 174 41

Box Boy 45

Patchwork Park 48

Ahead of the Game 52

Cutting-Room Floor 57

Sparkling Stars in Taupe 62

Friday-Night Special 66

County Fair 70

Fast Friends 74

Maggie's Star 79

Vintage LeMoyne Stars 84

Leap Year 90

ABOUT THE AUTHOR 95

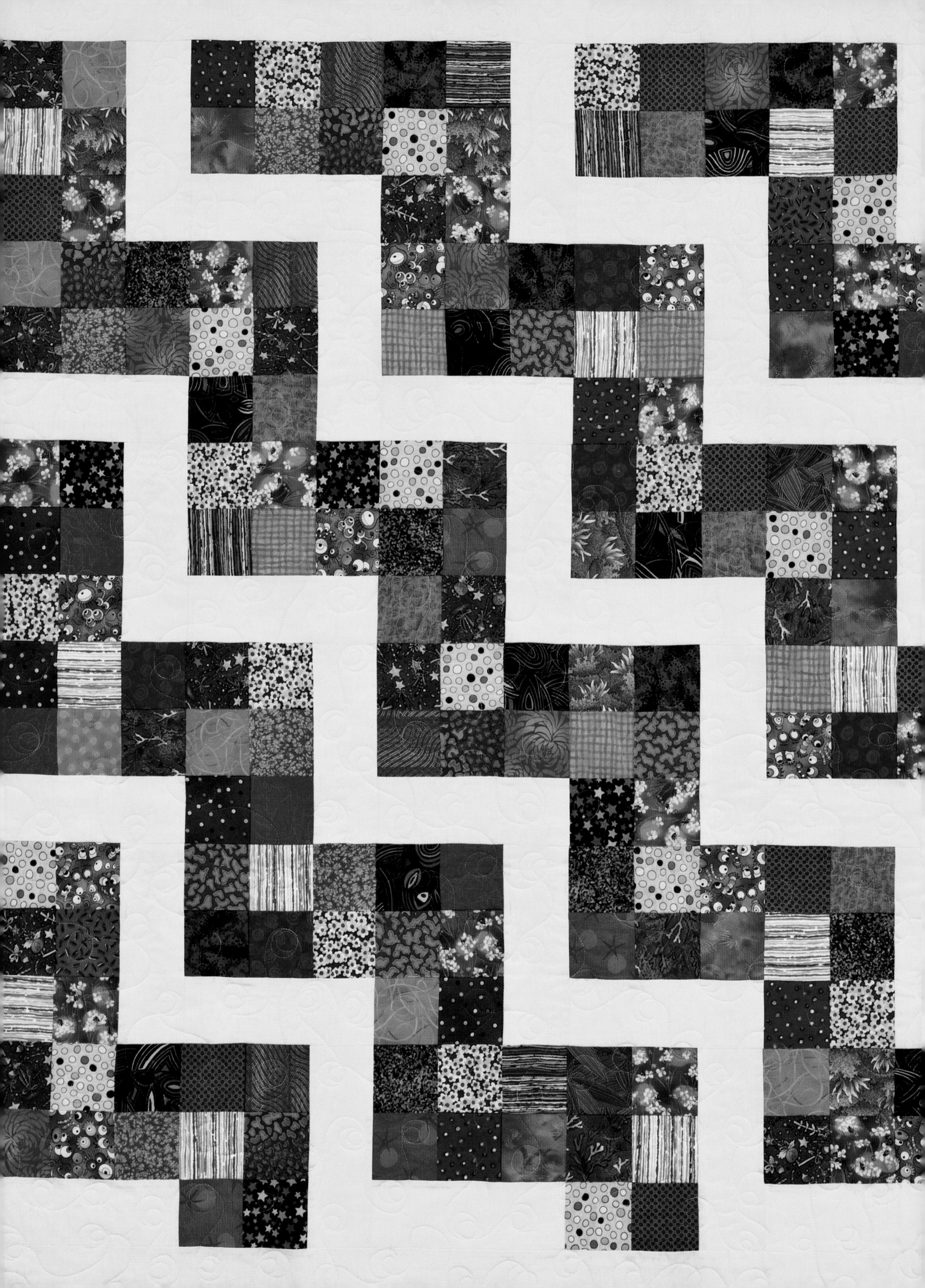

Introduction

Scrap quilts have long been a favorite of mine for many reasons. I love the way they look, I love the blend of different prints, colors, and textures, and I love making them. It's fun to choose fabrics, first at the quilt shop, and then from my stash, whether it's for one block at a time or for the whole quilt. And it's fun to watch the colors come together to form the design. I like to see if I can make the next block prettier than the last. And I like the ongoing challenge of seeing if I can make an ugly fabric look good. I like the idea of utilizing all those scraps I've saved that some people would deem useless. Your reasons may be different than mine, but it doesn't matter. If you have scraps, I'm happy to help you put them to use.

Selecting fabrics is another challenge for quilters that I'm happy to help you through. I'll explain how I consider the character, color, and contrast between prints to arrive at a nice homogenous blend of coordinated fabrics. I'll also discuss how to organize your scraps, and I'll give you tips for working smarter so you can get more quilts finished. I hesitate to suggest that you work more quickly, because I fear that haste will result in sloppiness. You can keep the fun in quilting and still do work you can be proud of.

Few basic quiltmaking skills are covered in this book because I thought that if you have scraps, you already know the basics. If you're still new to quilting, you may find it necessary to refer to another book with more details. If you're stalled at a beginner level, learning all about half-square triangles can take you to the next level. I explain the details of half-square and quarter-square triangles and how to cut them with special rulers. These skills are important to me and allow me to quickly produce the many quilts I make. I also include the important 1/4"-seam-allowance test. I've learned that using an accurate quilter's 1/4" seam allowance frees me to piece most any design I'm interested in.

Beginning and experienced quilters alike will enjoy the range of quilts I've included, from those that use fast, fun strip-piecing techniques to fussy quilts with set-in pieces like "Vintage LeMoyne Stars" (page 84). And if you're interested in trying something new, I've also included a few designs that use my Thirtysomething technique, and even one with my Twin Peaks technique. I hope you like them all!

–Gayle

Selecting **Scraps**

Most quilt patterns can be interpreted in scraps and are often enhanced because of them. Using multiple fabrics in one quilt adds texture, interest, and beauty.

There aren't any hard-and-fast rules when it comes to choosing fabric, but if you have trouble selecting fabrics for your quilts, then these tips should help. There are many people with wonderful color sense, and they're pretty good at breaking my rules. But the point is, these are the rules *I* follow. You can use them too if you like my style, or follow your instincts.

Character

When I started quilting more than 25 years ago, there weren't as many fabrics available. The only advice offered for choosing fabrics back then was that there should be contrast between the colors and a variety of print sizes and types should be included. Today, there are so many styles of fabric available that it has become harder to choose the right mix.

Quilters sometimes tell me they don't make scrap quilts because they have a hard time coordinating fabric. A coordinated color palette isn't mandatory, but in my opinion, the prettiest quilts are planned at least a little. You can easily choose fabrics that coordinate if you keep this little secret in mind: All colors work together if they relate to each other in character or style. Mixing too many styles will only result in chaos.

When you're selecting your fabrics, ask yourself what mood or feeling your fabric selection conveys. Are your fabrics elegant, funky, traditional, juvenile, or cute? Maybe they're romantic, bold, sophisticated, or sweet and innocent. Other styles or themes include 1800s or 1930s reproduction prints, plaids, batiks, and seasonal prints. Some fabrics blend easily with a variety of styles, while others are very specific and can be difficult to use in a scrap quilt. Be sure your choices convey the same style and weed out those that don't.

These fabrics represent a variety of different characters and do not work well together.

A simple trick to help choose prints that relate to each other is to select colors that have the same tint or undertones. Often they have the same character. Different fabrics may read as having a clear, bright hue; a muted, gray tone; a golden cast; or a brownish tinge. Step back 10 feet, and as long as the fabrics read the same, they'll work together in your quilt. It also helps to leave the room for a while and come back with fresh eyes; then you can quickly spot the fabrics that don't fit in. Your decision will ultimately be based on your own tastes and available fabric, so don't worry too much about your choices. After all, quilting is supposed to be fun.

One thing that I wouldn't do when selecting fabrics is use an "everything but the kitchen sink" approach. This is when you use anything just because you have it and want to use it up. Some prints can be difficult to use in a scrap quilt. If a fabric isn't working with your chosen palette, save it a little longer until more similar fabrics have accumulated, give it away, trade it, use it for rags, or throw it away!

Color

You'll also need to decide on a color palette. It's likely that your objective in making a scrap quilt is to thin your scrap bag a bit, so this is the obvious place to start. But there is no reason you can't dip into your main stash and cut a strip of this and a strip of that to round out the range of colors that you want in your quilt.

Sometimes we have so many options we don't know where to begin. See if one of these suggestions helps you decide.

- Choose the colors used in a favorite multicolored print.
- Use one of the bundles of fabric you've purchased and build a palette from it.
- Use the quilt recipient's favorite colors.
- Choose colors to coordinate with a specific room.
- Use the scraps in a color you have the most of, provided that they relate. Quilts made in a range of medium and dark prints in one color can be very attractive.

Contrast

In addition to deciding on the colors and character of your fabrics, you also need to consider their degree of lightness or darkness. This is usually referred to as a color's value. Any time a pattern instructs you to use light, medium, or dark fabrics, it's important that you follow the instructions carefully. If you don't, your quilt will not look the way you expect it to, because contrast is what makes the design distinguishable.

Busy, large-scale prints and high-contrast fabrics are popular now, but they can be some of the most difficult fabrics to work with because they often read both light *and* dark in the same patch. If your goal is to make the print stand out, showcase the fabric in a simple block and surround it with a contrasting solid fabric or a fabric that reads like a solid, like I did in "Make Momma Happy" (page 32). Blending many multicolored prints can also result in beautiful quilts, as long as fabrics with similar colors and styles are used.

I tend to like high contrast in my quilts and shy away from medium-toned fabrics. If not chosen carefully, medium-toned prints will blend with neighboring fabrics and disguise the design.

The medium tones work best when the darkest darks are placed with the darkest lights and the lightest lights are placed with the lightest darks.

As the quilt progresses, I like to put the blocks on my design wall to see if I need to tweak the fabric selection. I might want the quilt to read more blue. Or maybe I think a certain red hue would add the sparkle the quilt needs, or that a medium shade blends into the background too much. Some fabrics don't work as well as I'd like, so I replace the remaining pieces of that fabric. I don't hesitate to use my seam ripper. After all, it takes just a few minutes to rip, and I will be happier with the quilt.

When it's time to sew the quilt together, I arrange the blocks and check for even distribution of color. This isn't important to everyone; some quilters simply pick up blocks randomly when it's time to sew them together. The carefree approach to color placement appeals to them and can still produce fabulous quilts. Some wonderful examples of random placement can be found in antique quilts.

Being More **Productive**

When I first learned to quilt, I would joke that I had 300 quilts on my to-do list. Now I'm working on my second list of 300. I totally understand the desire to make quilts quickly. It's fun and exciting to try different fabric combinations, patterns, and techniques.

Recently, one gal in class said she needed tips to work more quickly. She was sitting next to someone who was content to sew so slowly that you could have counted the number of stitches per minute that she was taking. That's all right. There are no quilt police, and you won't get fined for quilting slowly. Besides, sometimes we want to work slowly because we want to do our best work. Other times we're trying a new technique and want to be sure we know what we're doing and want to avoid mistakes. I can't help you sew more quickly, but I can offer tips for being more productive.

Organize Your Scraps

Generally, scrap quilts take longer to make because handling so many different fabrics slows you down. Get your scraps organized; this is one of my best tips for being productive. Nearly every quilter I've ever met saves scraps from making quilts. For some, a 2" square will do; others won't save anything smaller than a 2½"-wide strip. No matter what size you save, as scraps accumulate, they soon become out of control unless you have a system for keeping them organized.

I sort and organize my scraps into boxes of common strip widths, squares, and triangles. I know many quilters do this and refer to it as a scrap-user system. Last winter I had surgery and wasn't comfortable cutting fabric for a while afterward. I was thrilled that I could still sew because my scraps were organized. My boxes of squares and triangles were ready and waiting, and they went into three different quilts in a matter of weeks.

Maybe the best advantage of keeping my scraps organized is the time it saves because I don't have to rummage through tangled, wrinkled scraps every time I want to make a scrap quilt, which is often. I find it's easier when I keep the pieces neat and flat; that way there's no need to iron those pieces again. I can simply take the box off the shelf, sort through it for the right color or value, and start sewing. I like to think of my boxes of organized scraps as a precut kit, only I haven't decided on the quilt pattern yet.

A neatly organized group of scraps is much more productive for creating quilts than an out-of-control mess.

Many quilters sort their scraps by color. This is great for your main stash, but I don't sort scraps by color. I rarely make a scrap quilt in a specific color and find I would have to sort through too many boxes for the size of scraps I needed from each box, plus I feel like I would inadvertently omit desirable colors for the palette I was developing.

Of course, organizing your scraps isn't mandatory. I'm sure many of you will ignore this advice and jump right into cutting your next quilt. You need to do what works for you, but I tend to think that getting everything in order will enable you to select fabrics for your scrap quilts more easily.

Cut Faster

Rotary cutters themselves are a time-saving tool, but these tips will ensure efficiency.

- Use a sharp blade in your rotary cutter. This will keep you from having to go back after each cut to get those last few threads that were skipped.
- Mark your ruler when cutting a quantity of strips the same width. A variety of repositionable strips, such as Glow-Line Tape or even painter's tape, are available to indicate the measurement. They help you align the ruler quickly and prevent error and eye fatigue.

- If at all possible, stack fabric when cutting. I generally cut four layers at once; any more, and the layers tend to shift slightly.

Sew Speedier

Again, the goal here isn't to be the fastest sewer, but there are some tricks that will save you time as you're piecing.

- Chain piece as you sew and always keep similar units oriented in the same direction as you sew, snip apart, *and* press. This will save you from having to rotate the pieces to determine which step you're on or what edge to sew next.

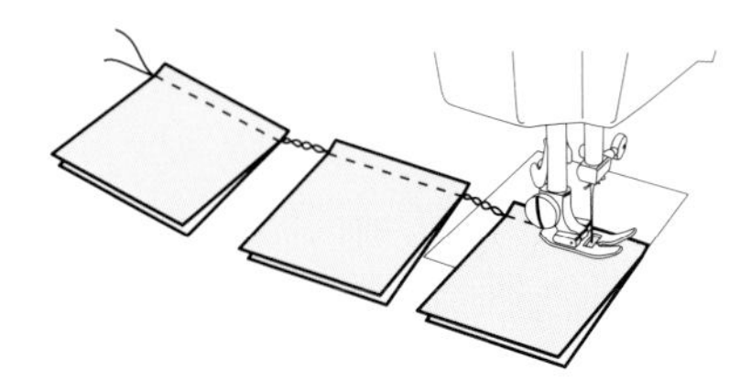

- Use a seam guide on the throat plate of your machine. Again, it will relieve eye strain and help you sew for longer periods of time and more quickly as you feed the fabric against the edge of the guide. Your machine may have come with a seam-guide attachment. If not, quilt shops generally carry seam-guide notions, or you can use several layers of masking tape to act as a built-up edge for feeding fabric.
- Obviously some designs go together more quickly than others. Random scrap quilts are faster to make than scrap quilts where each block uses different fabrics. Cutting one block at a time slows you down and it can be confusing to keep track of which fabrics belong in which block. And with scraps placed randomly, you can often use fun strip-piecing techniques to speed things along a bit.

  Randomly selecting pieces to sew next to each other can sometimes slow you down. Rather than letting you labor over the decision, some quilting teachers suggest that you put all your cut pieces into a paper bag and use whatever you pull out of the bag next. This is fine, provided you made good choices about what goes into the bag. Personally I think it's more fun to choose which prints will be next to each other. I often imagine that the fabrics I have sewn together into a small unit for the quilt would make a gorgeous quilt with just those fabrics. So rather than fret about which pieces to sew together, try to enjoy the process. You already made your fabric selection. Now just be careful that you don't repeatedly sew the same prints together.
- Rather than piecing one block at a time, sew the same units for all the blocks at the same time. The advantage here is that once you figure something out, you'll save time if you repeat the action right away. So if you find one step confusing, you'll get into a rhythm, and you won't have to stop to rethink that step every time you come back to it like you would if you were making individual blocks. This is why I encourage my students to try to get back to their class project as soon as possible after class if the technique was new to them.
- You can skip laying out the pieces for each block when you sew the same step for each block at one time. To check that they're correctly arranged as you sew, compare the next two pieces with the last two you sewed. They should be arranged the same way under the presser foot.
- Do you ever have trouble getting motivated to begin sewing, but once you've started you're fine? Try this trick a friend taught me years ago. Stop sewing in the middle of a seam! Of course this only works if you can leave your machine set up all the time. Somehow the simple act of sewing the few inches left in a seam is all it takes to put me back in the groove. You might also try leaving piles of patchwork lined up and ready to go.
- If you're serious about making lots of quilts, it's worthwhile to invest in learning the how and why of different techniques. Focus on a few to master, taking classes that emphasize the process rather than just making the project. You will work smarter and faster with the knowledge gained.

Quiltmaking **Techniques**

The projects in this book use basic rotary-cutting techniques that are familiar to most quilters. This section covers a minimum of quiltmaking skills necessary to complete your quilt. Mastering these skills and knowing your equipment will make the time you spend constructing quilts more efficient and enjoyable.

Cutting Triangles

Next to squares and rectangles, right triangles are most often seen in traditional patchwork designs. Two types of right triangles are commonly used: half-square triangles (squares cut in half) and quarter-square triangles (squares cut into quarters). It's important to know how to recognize them and their differences. Once you understand the math behind cutting triangles, hundreds of patterns are possible. Quilting has few hard-and-fast rules, but one that is rarely broken is that the straight of grain of the fabric should run along the outside edges of the block. If the cut bias edge of a triangle were at the edge of the block, it would cause the block to stretch and distort and be difficult to handle.

Half-square triangles. If the straight of grain is on the short edge of the triangle, it's a half-square triangle. The short side is the finished measurement you would know.

Quarter-square triangles. If the straight of grain is on the long edge of the triangle, it's a quarter-square triangle. The long side is the finished measurement you would know.

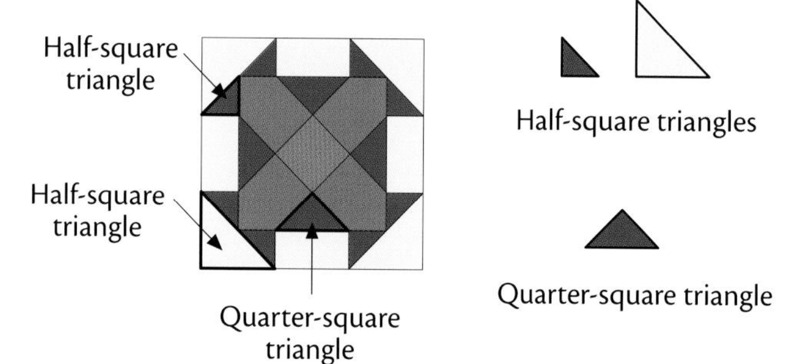

When it comes to cutting and sewing right triangles, you have a lot of options. The most common method cuts triangles from squares. My favorite method when using scraps, however, is to use a ruler designed specifically for cutting triangles. I'll cover both methods here.

Cutting Triangles Using Traditional Methods

This is the method you see most often used in quilting instructions. Because most people are familiar with this technique and it requires no special tool, the cutting instructions for the projects in this book are written for this method. You'll start by cutting squares, and then either cut them in half diagonally or into quarters diagonally to create the triangles.

Half-square triangles. If you were to draft a template for a half-square triangle with a 1/4" seam allowance all around, you would see that at the square corner, the cut edge is 1/4" away from the sewn or finished edge. Yet at the pointy corners, there is 5/8" difference between the cut and finished points. Adding 1/4" and 5/8" gives you 7/8". Measure the length of the triangle's short edge because this is the direction the fabric grain line runs in a half-square triangle.

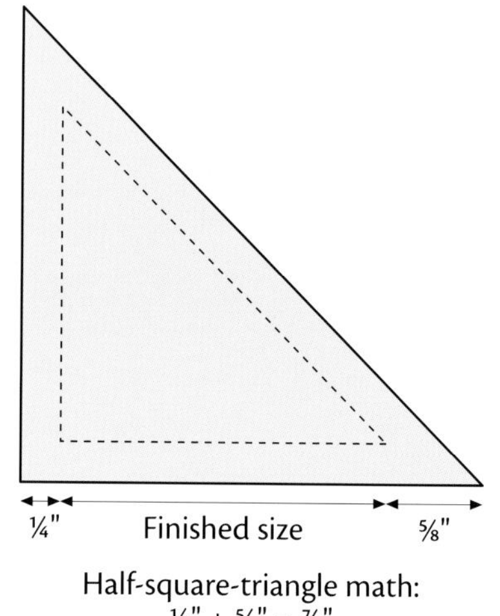

Half-square-triangle math:
1/4" + 5/8" = 7/8"

The rule or formula to cut half-square triangles is to add 7/8" to the finished measurement of the short edge, cut squares to this size, and then cut the squares in half diagonally.

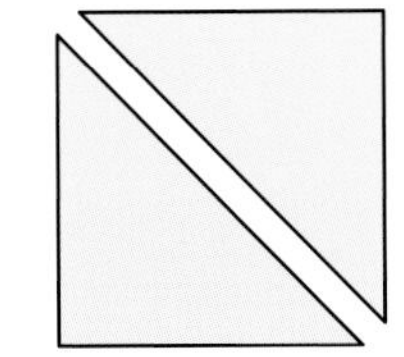

Finished size + 7/8" = square cut size

Quarter-square triangles. If you were to draft a template for a quarter-square triangle with a 1/4" seam allowance all around, you would see that at both pointy corners there is 5/8" difference between the cut and finished points. Adding 5/8" plus 5/8" gives you 1 1/4". We measure across the long edge because this is the direction the grain line runs in a quarter-square triangle.

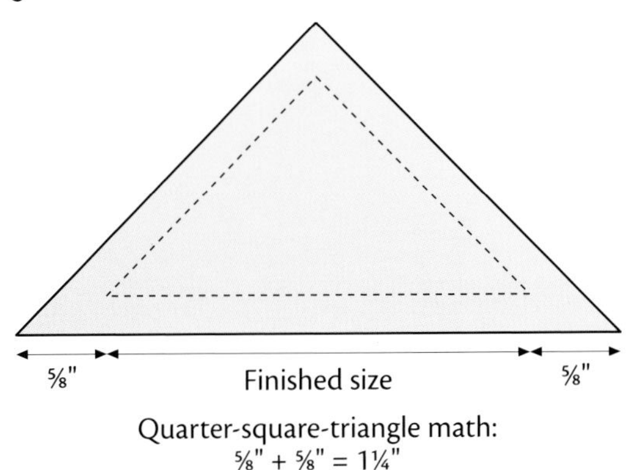

Quarter-square-triangle math:
5/8" + 5/8" = 1 1/4"

The rule or formula to cut quarter-square triangles is to add 1 1/4" to the finished measurement of the long side of the triangle, cut squares to this size, and then cut the squares into quarters diagonally. For example, if you wanted a quarter-square triangle to finish 4" along the long edge, cut a 5 1/4" square and cut it into quarters diagonally.

Finished size + 1 1/4" = square cut size

Cutting Triangles Using a Triangle-Cutting Ruler

There are several rotary-cutting rulers designed specifically for cutting half-square and quarter-square triangles. The benefit of these rulers is that they all work on the same principle: *Pieces that finish at the same width can be cut from the same width.* In other words, you can cut squares, rectangles, *and* triangles from the same-width strip because the formula for adding a seam allowance is to add 1/2" for all these pieces. This minimizes the amount of fabric you use and the time it takes to cut different-size strips.

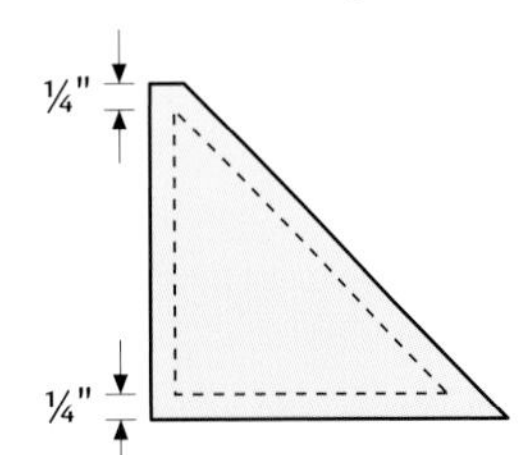

Half-square-triangle math:
1/4" + 1/4" + finished size = strip width

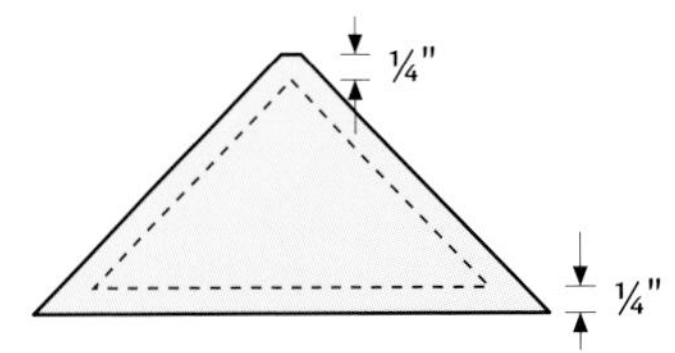

Quarter-square-triangle math:
1/4" + 1/4" + finished size = strip width

Several brands of triangle-cutting rulers are available to cut either half-square or quarter-square triangles. Some rulers can cut both half- and quarter-square triangles, but most rulers are specific to one or the other. Look for these rulers under such names as Easy Angle, Companion

Angle, Omnigrid 96, Omnigrid 98, All-In-One Ruler™, and Quilter's Rule QRT-6. I highly recommend you get rulers for cutting each type of triangle (or dig them out of your closet) and learn how to use them. Keep in mind they're all marked differently, so follow the instructions for your ruler until you become familiar with it.

In general, to cut half-square triangles using these rulers, start with a strip of fabric ½" wider than the finished side of the triangle. Place the ruler on the strip of fabric so that the extra ⅜" at the top point of the ruler extends past the upper edge of the fabric. If the ruler has a blunted tip, it's blunted at ⅜", and then that edge is placed at the upper edge of the strip. Line up the lower edge of the strip with the correct line on the ruler. Be sure you read your ruler's instructions, because on some rulers the number corresponds with the strip width while on other rulers it corresponds to the triangle finished size. Cut along both edges of the triangle, and then rotate the triangle ruler and align it upside down on the strip. Continue rotating the ruler and cutting across the strip until you have the number of triangles you want.

Generally instructions for cutting quarter-square triangles using these rulers are basically the same. Start with a strip of fabric ½" wider than the finished height of the triangle. Proper placement of the quarter-square triangle ruler on the strip will result in triangles with the tip blunted ⅛".

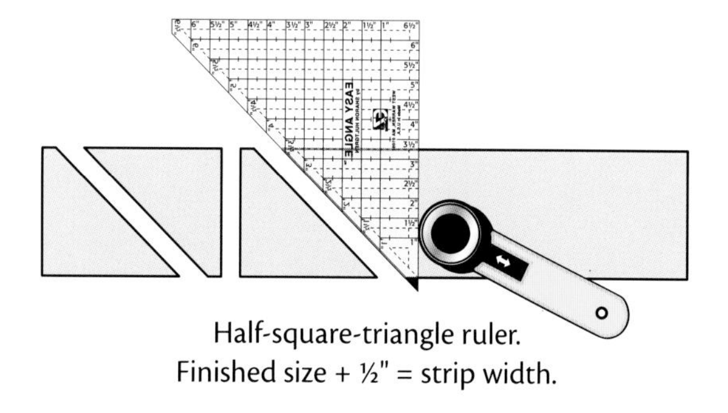

Half-square-triangle ruler.
Finished size + ½" = strip width.

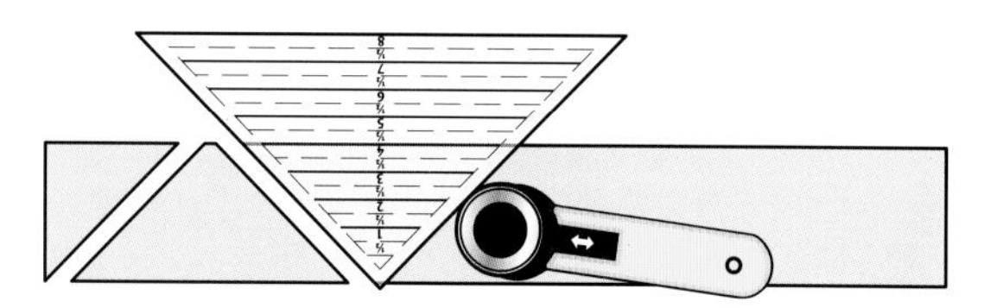

Quarter-square-triangle ruler.
Finished size + ½" = strip width.

Cutting Trapezoids

Keep the rules for cutting triangles in mind if you need trapezoids. Imagine that a trapezoid is a decapitated triangle. The strip-width rule still applies, and so does the triangle formula, depending on the type of trapezoid you're cutting. The double trapezoid units in "Box Boy" (page 45) are cut from a strip set using a half-square-triangle ruler.

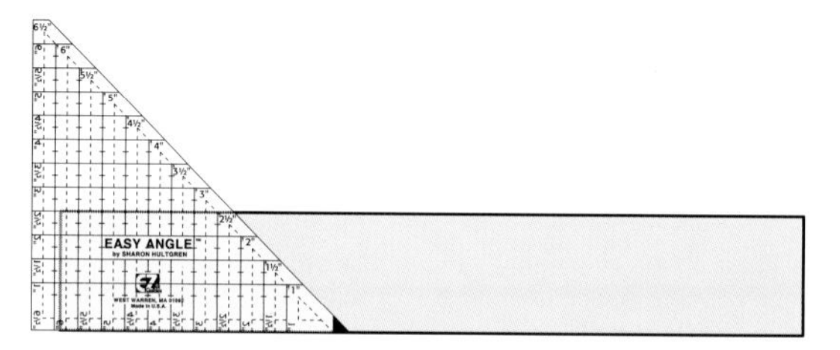

The formula for using this tool to cut trapezoids is to add ⅞" to the longest finished edge.

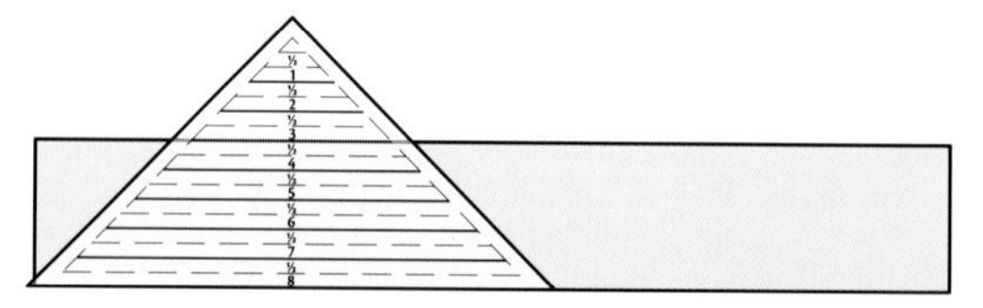

The formula for using this tool to cut trapezoids is to add 1¼" to the longest finished edge.

Sewing

Measurements for all strips and individual pieces include the quilter's ¼" seam allowance. Likewise, sewing using the quilter's scant ¼" seam allowance is required for all template-free quilt patterns. Sewing accurately is more about the result than how the seam allowance actually measures. We use a scant ¼" so the patchwork will finish the correct size and all the pieces fit together. If you've had trouble in the past getting your pieces to fit, follow these steps to see how you need to adjust your seam allowance to achieve perfect patchwork.

Cut three pieces of fabric, each 1½" x 5". Sew the three pieces together along the long edges using a ¼" seam allowance. Press and measure the width of the three-strip unit. It should now measure exactly 3½" wide, with the center strip measuring 1". Repeat the test if necessary using a slightly wider or narrower seam allowance until you find the correct width.

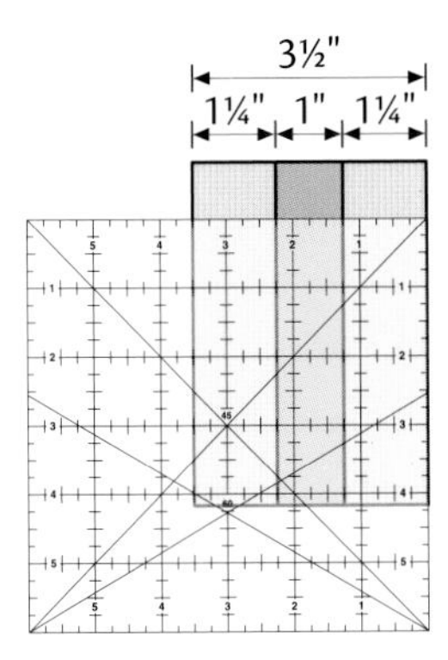

Once you've found where to properly position your fabric edge to achieve the correct seam allowance, mark the position on the throat plate of your sewing machine with several layers of masking tape. Even if your presser foot is an accurate ¼" or you can adjust the needle position, you'll find the tape helpful. I find many students have a habit of guiding their fabric along the wrong guide. Repeat the test with the tape in place to be certain you've positioned it accurately.

Controlling Bias

Bias does not stretch out of shape until after it's been cut. You can minimize the stretching if you press the fabric using heavy spray starch before you cut any triangles. Stretching can occur when either sewing or pressing.

When sewing any two pieces together, don't hold them back. Just let the machine feed them under the needle. You are merely "steering" them through straight. If you have a tendency to stretch the bias edges, you may be holding on too tightly. The bias may also be stretched as you press. Press gently, gliding the iron in the direction of the threads in the fabric, allowing the heat of the iron to do the work.

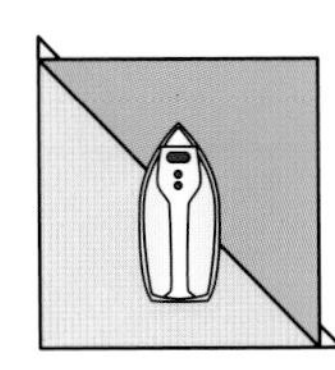

Like this.

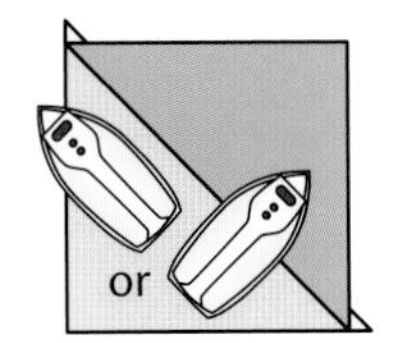

Not like this.

Adding Borders

Borders are more than just an easy way to make a quilt larger without extra piecing. They also frame the design and help calm the activity of all the different fabrics.

Don't be tempted to simply apply the border strips to each edge without measuring. If you skip this important step, you could add several inches more to one side than the other. Extra fabric in the border is not easily quilted out and can result in wavy or rippling borders or a quilt that doesn't have squared edges and won't lie flat.

Border strips are generally cut across the width of the fabric, selvage to selvage, and joined end to end when necessary to achieve the required length. Backstitch these short seams and press the seam allowances open so they lie flat and are less conspicuous. Try to place the seams randomly around the quilt to make them even less noticeable.

Follow these instructions to add borders to your quilt.

1. Measure the width of the quilt top through the center and along the two edges parallel to the center to find the average width. I measure using the actual border strip, rather than a ruler or tape measure. I mark the lengths on one strip with a pin and compare the three lengths. Then I cut two border strips to the average length.

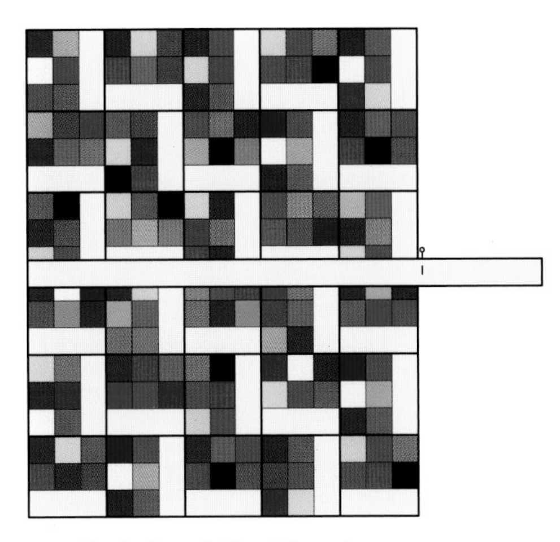

Mark the width with a pin.

2. Fold the two border strips in half and mark their centers with pins.
3. Fold the quilt in half in both directions and mark the center of each edge with a pin.
4. Matching the centers, sew the borders to the top and bottom edges of your quilt. Press the seam allowances toward the border strips.
5. Repeat the process to measure the length of the quilt top, including the borders just added, and find the average measurement. Cut the borders to the required length and sew them to the sides of the quilt top.

Mark the length with a pin.

Finishing Techniques

The quilt top is done—now it's time to make it a real quilt! Suggested quilting designs are included with each project, but feel free to change the design to suit your taste.

Backing

The yardage required for the quilt backings for the patterns in this book are based on 42"-wide fabric unless otherwise indicated. Plan to make the backing at least 3" larger than the quilt top on each side. For large quilts, it's usually necessary to sew two or three widths of the backing together to make a backing the required size. Remove the selvages from the backing fabric and use a ½" seam allowance to sew the widths together. Press the seam allowances open. I like to use extra-wide 108" backing fabric so I can avoid this step. If you're sending your quilt to a long-arm quilter, find out what her requirements are before determining the backing size needed.

Basting

Basting a quilt for a long-arm quilter isn't required; layering the quilt is part of the long-arm quilting process. If you intend to quilt by hand, I suggest thread basting. If you're quilting with your home sewing machine, pin basting works better so that you don't inadvertently stitch your basting threads in place with your quilting stitches.

To begin, secure the backing, wrong side up, on a flat surface using masking tape to keep it flat and taut but not stretched. Spread the batting over the backing. Next spread the quilt top over the batting, making sure that all layers stay smooth and even. Position the top to leave at least 3" of extra backing and batting on each side. Make long basting stitches in horizontal and vertical rows 4" apart, or pin baste every 4", avoiding areas where you plan to quilt. For example, pin in the center of the square rather than across the seams if you first plan to stitch in the ditch.

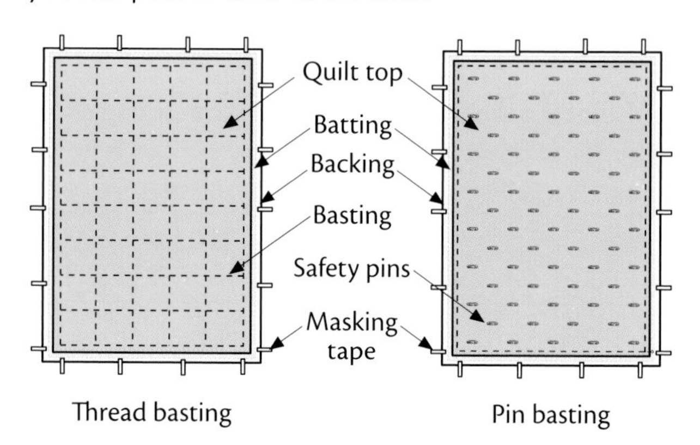

Thread basting Pin basting

When pin basting, I first insert the safety pins and leave them open; then I remove the tape holding the quilt backing in place. Finally, I close the pins. With less tension on the fabric they're easier to close.

Quilting

I like to machine quilt using cotton thread that matches the quilt top. First, I do straight-line quilting or quilt in the ditch at least in the seams between the blocks. This type of quilting is easiest to do using a walking foot to help feed the three quilt layers evenly through the machine without them shifting and puckering. Finally, I add any curved quilting designs using a darning foot with the feed dogs dropped or covered. Try different threads, needles, and machine tension to see what works best with the fabric and batting you're using. Experimenting with identical scraps is also great for practicing new designs and as a warm-up exercise. The goal is smooth lines in the design with consistently sized stitches and even tension.

Many excellent books are available to help you perfect your quilting skills, but if at all possible, I suggest you take a class. Not only are classes inspiring and more fun than teaching yourself, but you can learn much from the experiences of others.

Binding

After completing the quilting, machine baste in the seam allowance at the edge of the quilt. Trim the batting and backing even with the quilt top and bind the quilt following these steps.

1. Cut the number of 2¼"-wide strips required to finish the quilt. The binding needs to be at least 10" longer than the quilt perimeter. Cut each end of the strips at a 45° angle. Join all the strips end to end and press the seam allowances open. Fold and press the binding in half lengthwise, wrong sides together.

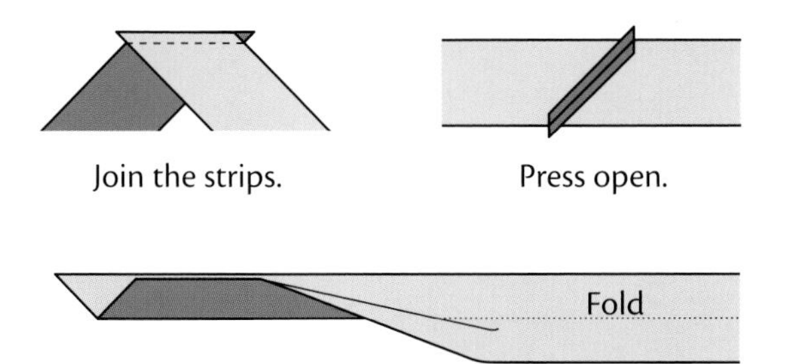

Join the strips.

Press open.

Fold lengthwise and press.

2. With the raw edges aligned, place the binding strip on top of your layered quilt, beginning about 20" from the corner of the quilt. Using a ¼" seam allowance, start stitching about 6" from the end of the binding. Sew through both layers of binding and all three layers of the quilt. Keep the edges of the binding even with the edge of the quilt top. Stop stitching ¼" from the corner and backstitch. Remove the quilt from under the presser foot.

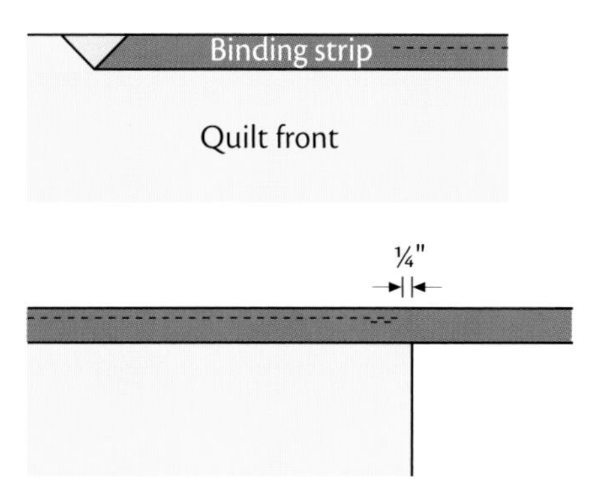

3. Turn the quilt to sew the binding to the adjacent edge. Fold the binding strip up to be even with the right edge of the quilt, and then fold the strip down to form a pleat, placing the fold even with the top edge of the quilt. Keep the raw edges of the binding and the quilt top even. Begin stitching again on the other side of the pleat, ¼" from the edge, and continue to ¼" from the next corner. Repeat these steps until all corners are sewn.

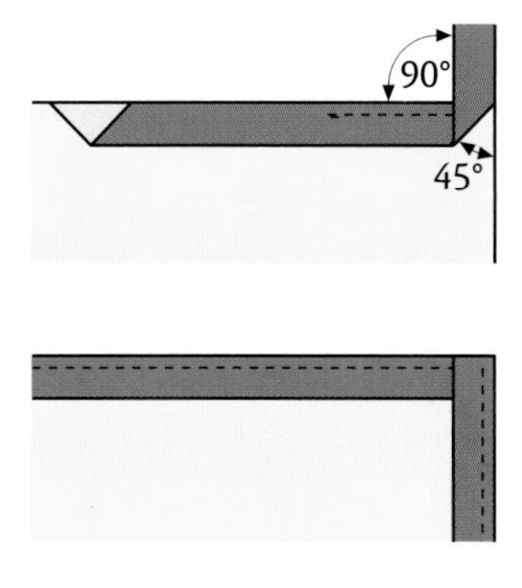

4. When you're about 8" from where you began attaching the binding, unfold the beginning and end of the strip and lap the beginning of the strip over the end of the strip. Draw a line on the tail next to the 45° cut of the starting end. Draw another line ½" away, toward the end of the tail, making the binding ½" longer. Cut on the second line.

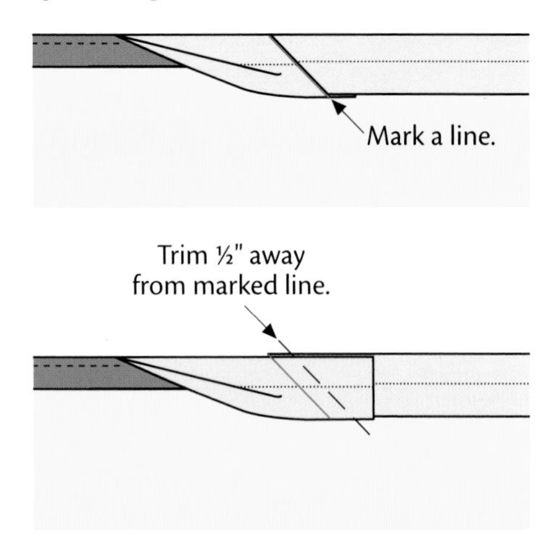

5. Pin the ends of the binding right sides together. Sew using a ¼" seam allowance. Finger-press the seam allowances open. Refold the binding and finish stitching it to the quilt.

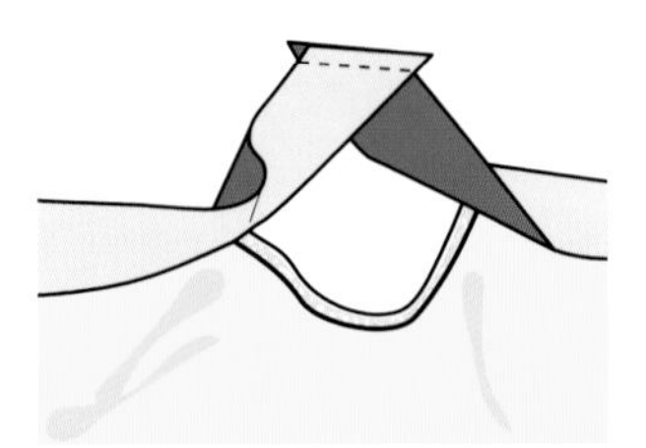

6. Turn the folded edge of the binding to the back of the quilt so it covers the row of machine stitching. Stitch the binding in place with thread that matches the binding. At each corner, fold the binding to form a miter. If I quilted by hand, I sew the binding down by hand with a blind stitch; if I quilted by machine, I sew it down by machine. To finish by machine, use an open-toe presser foot, thread to match the border (or clear) on top, and thread to match the binding in the bobbin. With the quilt right side up, stitch in the ditch (the seam line between border and binding), catching the binding on the back. Stitch the miters closed by hand.

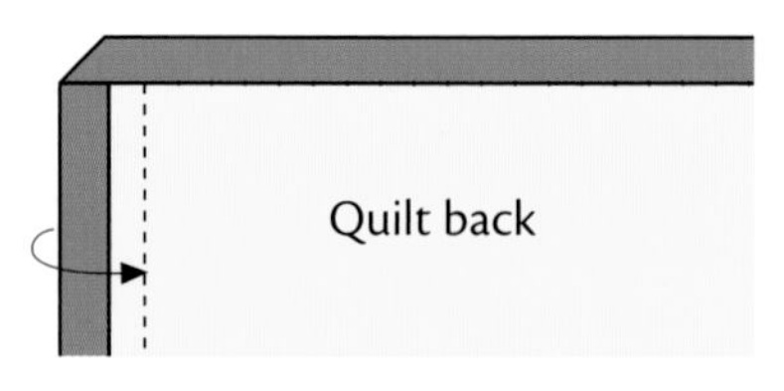

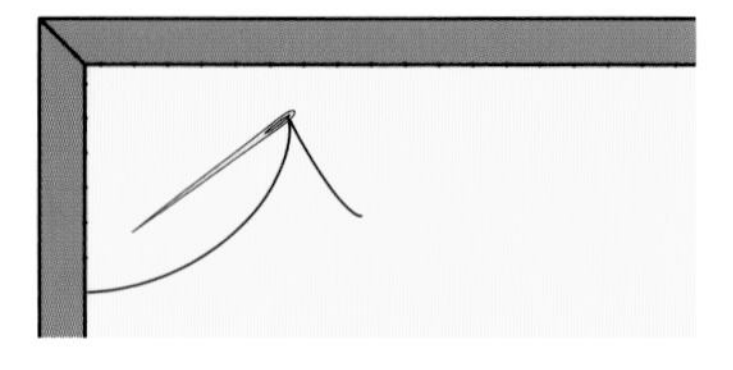

Signing Your Quilt

At the very least, be sure to sign and date your completed quilt with a permanent fabric-marking pen. If you want to do something more elaborate, you can make and attach a quilt label, including information such as the name of the quilt, your name, the date the quilt was completed, and the name of the person the quilt was made for. Consider making the label from a light-colored scrap of fabric that you've also used in the quilt top.

Displaying your Quilts

Quilts covering the walls will add warmth and character to your home. Okay, maybe one quilt will do. Just because I have them in every room in my home doesn't mean you have to. If you choose to hang a quilt, there are several options. Quilt hangers are available that grip the edge of the quilt. The hangers are permanently mounted on the wall. Another option is to hang the quilt from a curtain rod in a pocket or sleeve attached to the back of the quilt. I add sleeves after the quilt has been bound. Following is my method for making sleeves.

1. Cut a strip of fabric as long as the width of your quilt and 9" wide. This will make a 4"-wide sleeve. To make a deeper sleeve, double the desired finished width and add 1" for seam allowances. If, for example, you wish to add a 5"-wide sleeve, cut the fabric strip 11" wide. If you plan to enter your quilt in a show, check the specifications for attaching a sleeve. A 4"-wide sleeve is often required, but standards may differ from one quilt show to another.
2. On each short end of the strip, fold over ½", and then fold ½" again to make a hem. Press and stitch by machine. Fold the strip in half lengthwise, wrong sides together, raw edges aligned and press.

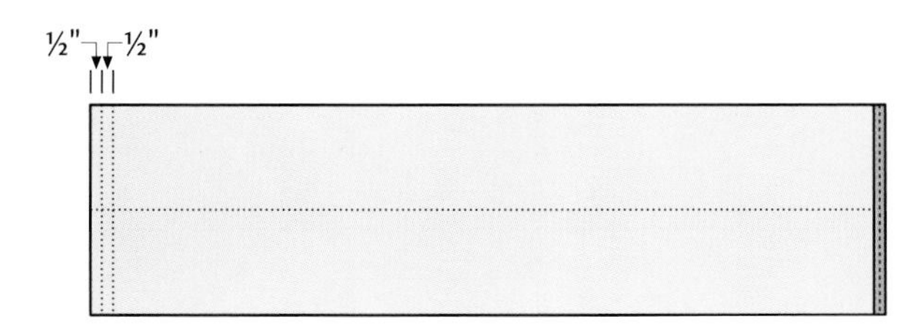

3. Place the sleeve on the back of the quilt so that the folded edge extends beyond the front of the quilt and the raw edges of the sleeve are 1" below the binding. With the quilt right side up and using thread that matches the outer border, machine stitch in the ditch between the binding and border.

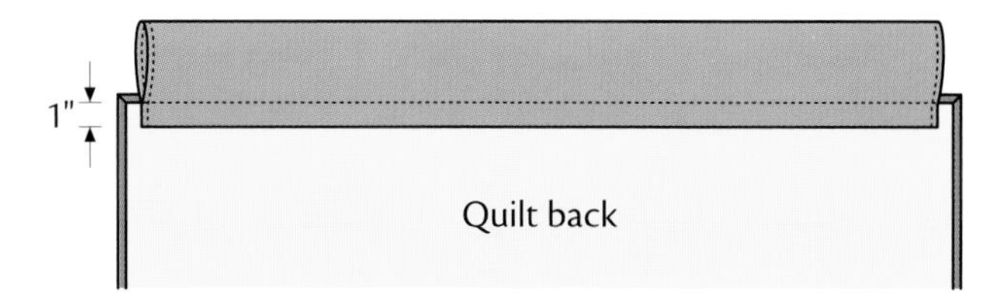

4. Pin the folded edge of the sleeve to the back of the quilt, pushing the edge up about ¼" to allow a little extra room for the hanging rod. This will help the front of the quilt to hang smoothly. Blindstitch the sleeve to the back of the quilt, being careful to only sew through the batting and backing.

22
25
28
32

52
57
62
66

The **Projects**

Joy in the Morning

Pieced and quilted by Gayle Bong

Finished quilt: 51½" x 60½"

Finished block: 9"

Materials

Yardages are based on 42"-wide fabric.

2 yards *total* of assorted bright scraps for blocks

1½ yards of light yellow solid fabric for blocks and border

½ yard of fabric for binding

3½ yards of fabric for backing

58" x 67" piece of batting

The sunny yellow in this quilt reminds me of a summer morning when the garden is alive with color. I created this simple design for my lady friends to make for charity quilts. It begins with a quick strip-piecing technique using 3½" strips. If you prefer, you may start with 3½" squares. Choose your scraps first, and then find the perfect background color to show them off.

Cutting		
Please read all the instructions before starting.		
FABRIC	FIRST CUT	FOLLOWING CUT
Assorted bright scraps	36 strips, 3½" x 21", or 180 squares, 3½" x 3½"	
Light yellow solid	8 strips, 3½" x 42"	30 rectangles, 3½" x 9½"
	6 strips, 3½" x 42"	
Binding fabric	6 strips, 2¼" x 42"	

Making the Blocks

After sewing each seam, press the seam allowances in the direction indicated by the arrows.

1. Sew pairs of bright print 3½" strips together along the long edges to make 18 strip sets. Press the seam allowances to either side. Crosscut the strip sets into 90 segments, 3½" wide. If you're starting with squares, sew pairs together into 90 units.

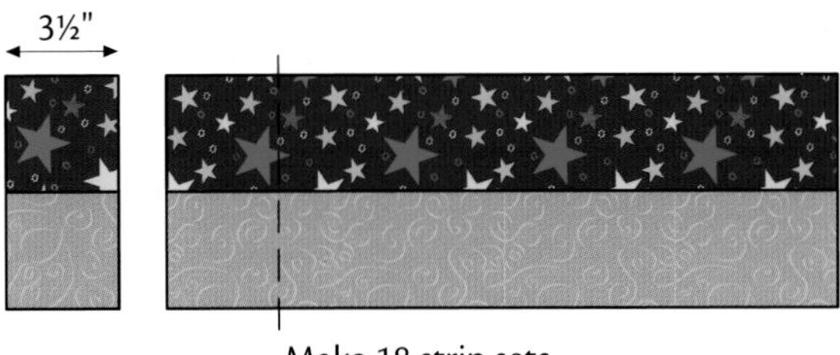

Make 18 strip sets.
Cut 90 segments.

2. Sew two units from step 1 together to make a four-patch unit. You may need to re-press one of the seams so the seam allowances alternate directions. Sew another pair of bright squares to any edge of the four-patch unit. Make 30 six-patch units.

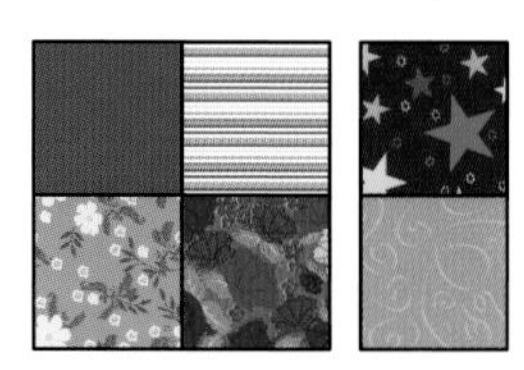

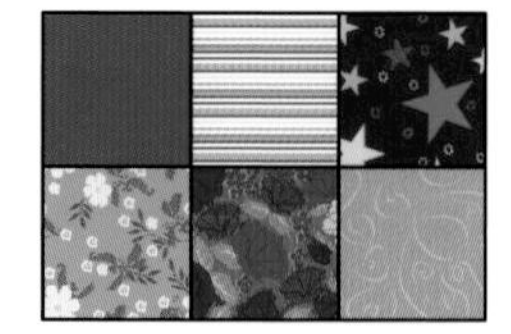

Make 30.

3. Sew a light yellow rectangle to either long edge of each six-patch unit to complete the blocks.

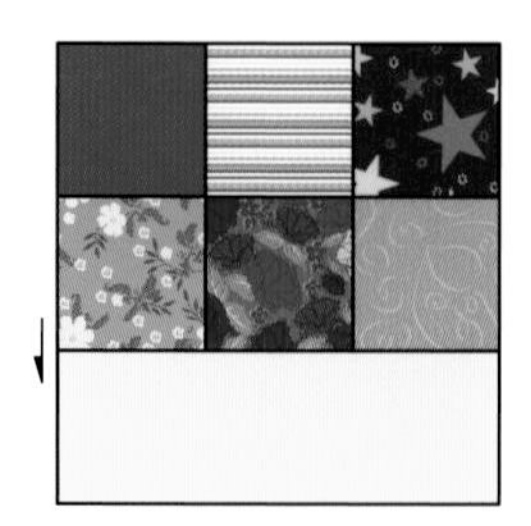

Make 30.

Assembling the Quilt Top

1. Arrange the blocks in six rows of five blocks each, rotating them as shown to create the zigzag pattern. Sew the blocks into rows, and then sew the rows together.
2. Attach the yellow 3½"-wide border strips to the quilt, referring to "Adding Borders" on page 15 to measure, cut, and sew them.

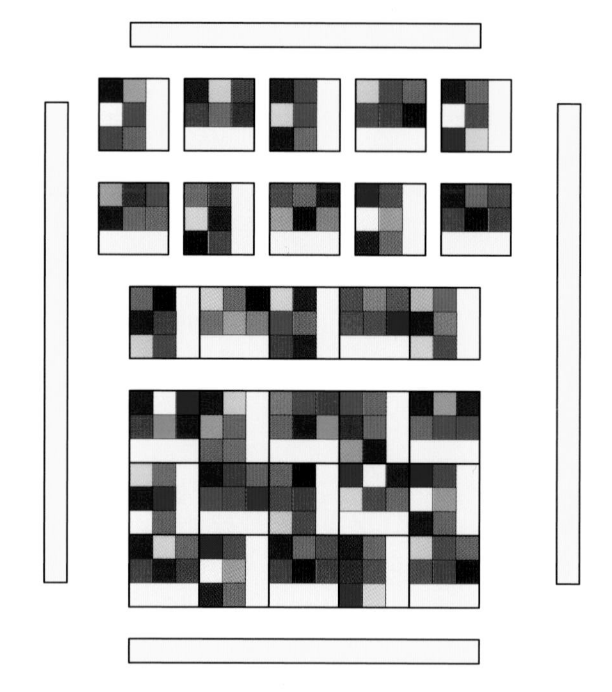

Quilt assembly

Finishing the Quilt

Refer to "Finishing Techniques" on page 16 for detailed instructions.

1. Layer the quilt top with the batting and backing; baste.
2. Hand or machine quilt. I quilted a pantograph design (a design that goes from one edge to the other with no breaks) on my quilt. Any fun, easy, meandering pattern is ideal for machine quilting this quilt.
3. Use the 2¼"-wide strips to bind the edges of your quilt.

Autumn Applause

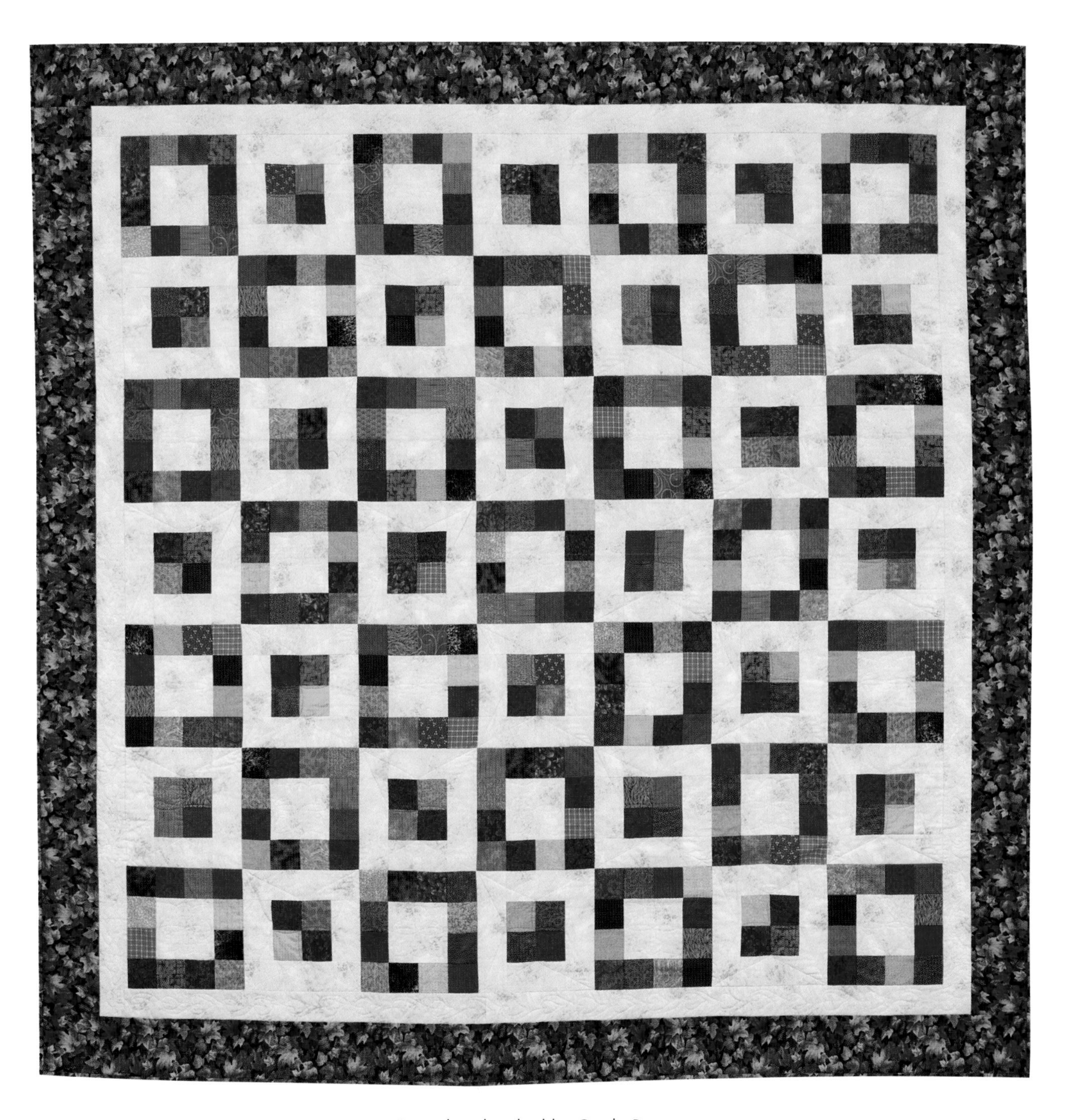

Pieced and quilted by Gayle Bong

Finished quilt: 85½" x 85½"

Finished block: 10"

Materials

Yardages are based on 42"-wide fabric except where noted.

3⅜ yards of light gold fabric for block backgrounds and inner border

3 yards *total* of assorted medium and dark scraps in red, green, gold, and rust for blocks

2⅛ yards of dark print for outer border and binding

2¾ yards of 108"-wide fabric for backing

90" x 90" piece of batting

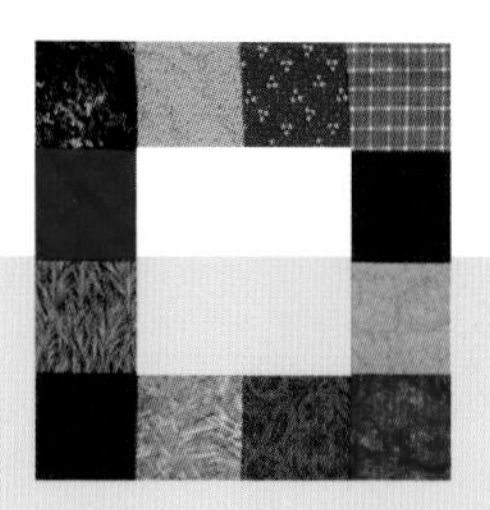

This is my version of a square-in-a-square design assembled with fast and fun strip piecing. Using a light gold background gives this quilt a traditional look. I used a very controlled palette, but this design is equally effective with a broader range of colors. It's also easily adaptable to other strip sizes.

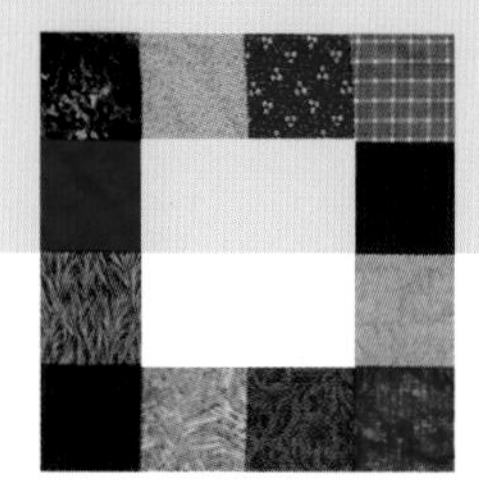

Cutting		
Please read all the instructions before starting.		
FABRIC	FIRST CUT	FOLLOWING CUT
Light gold	4 strips, 5½" x 42"	25 squares, 5½" x 5½"
	7 strips, 3" x 42"	48 rectangles, 3" x 5½"
	4 strips, 10½" x 42"	48 rectangles, 3" x 10½"
	8 strips, 3" x 42"	
Assorted medium and dark scraps	72 strips, 3" x 21"	
Dark print	9 strips, 5½" x 42"	
	9 strips, 2¼" x 42"	

Making Block A

After sewing each seam, press the seam allowances in the direction indicated by the arrows.

1. Sew pairs of medium and dark 3" x 21" strips together along the long edges to make 36 strip sets. Press the seam allowances to either side. Sew two pairs of strip sets together, staggering the ends about 10" as shown. Press the seam allowances to either side. Make 18 staggered strip sets. Crosscut the strip sets into segments, 3" wide. Cut 98 two-square segments and 50 four-square segments. Set aside 48 assorted two-square segments for block B.

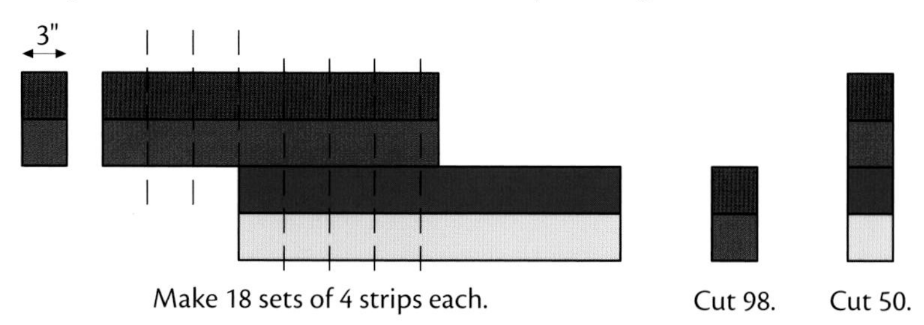

Make 18 sets of 4 strips each. Cut 98. Cut 50.

2. Sew two-square segments to opposite sides of each light gold 5½" square. Sew four-square segments to the other two sides of each square to complete the blocks. Make 25 blocks.

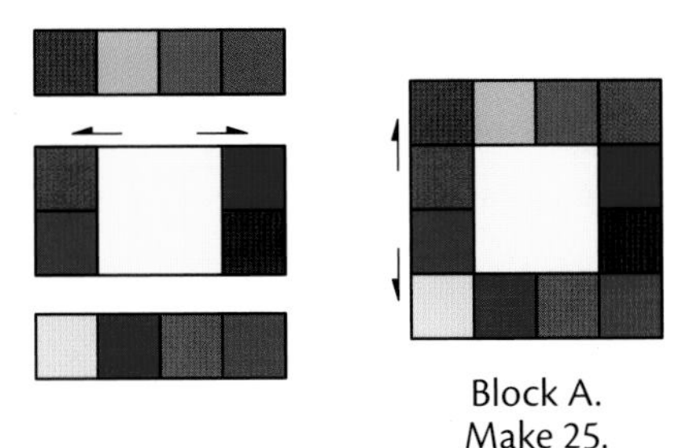

Block A.
Make 25.

Making Block B

1. Sew together pairs of the two-square units set aside in step 1 of "Making Block A" to make 24 four-patch units. Press the seam allowances in either direction.

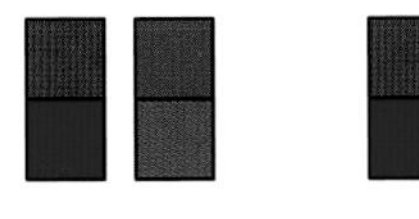

Make 24.

2. Sew light gold 3" x 5½" rectangles to opposite sides of each four-patch unit. Sew light gold 3" x 10½" rectangles to the other two sides of each unit to complete the blocks. Make 24 blocks.

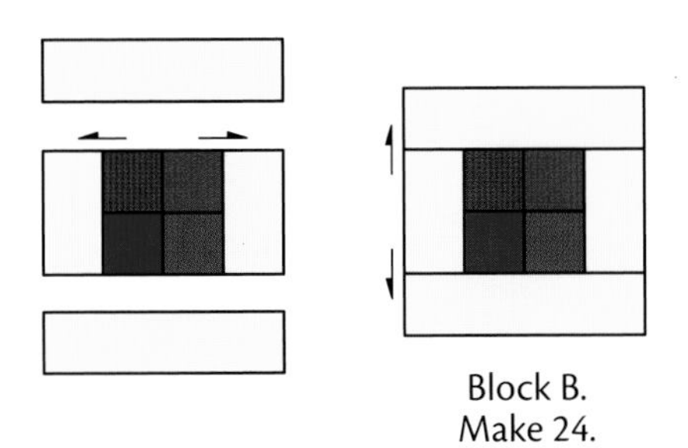

Block B.
Make 24.

Assembling the Quilt Top

1. Refer to the quilt assembly diagram above right to arrange the blocks in seven rows of seven blocks each, alternating blocks A and B in each row and from row to row. Play with the position of the blocks until you're happy with the color arrangement. Sew the blocks into rows, and then sew the rows together.

2. Attach the light gold 3"-wide inner-border strips to the quilt top, referring to "Adding Borders" on page 15 to measure, cut, and sew them. Repeat with the dark print 5½"-wide outer-border strips.

Quilt assembly

Finishing the Quilt

Refer to "Finishing Techniques" on page 16 for detailed instructions.

1. Layer the quilt top with the batting and backing; baste.
2. Hand or machine quilt. Follow the quilting suggestions shown below or use your own design.

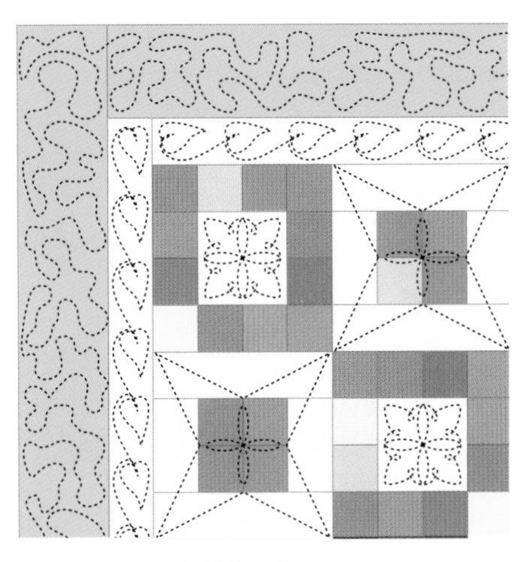

Quilting diagram

3. Use the dark print 2¼"-wide strips to bind the edges of your quilt.

Confused Nine Patch

Pieced and quilted by Gayle Bong

Finished quilt: 82½" x 94½"

Finished A and B blocks: 6"

Finished border block: 4" x 6"

Materials

Yardages are based on 42"-wide fabric except where noted.

3 yards of dark blue tone-on-tone fabric for blocks, pieced first border, second border, and binding

3 yards *total* of assorted pastel fabrics for blocks and pieced third border

2⅛ yards of cream fabric for block backgrounds

2 yards of dark blue print for fourth border

2½ yards of 108"-wide fabric for backing

90" x 102" piece of batting

Cutting		
Please read all the instructions before starting.		
FABRIC	FIRST CUT	FOLLOWING CUT
Assorted pastels	72 strips, 2½" x 21"	
Cream	9 strips, 2½" x 42"	Crosscut 1 strip in half to make 2 strips, 2½" x 21"
	4 strips, 6½" x 42"	20 squares, 6½" x 6½"
	3 strips, 6½" x 42"	18 rectangles, 4½" x 6½"
	4 squares, 4½" x 4½"	
Dark blue tone-on-tone	20 strips, 2½" x 42"	Crosscut 16 strips in half to make 32 strips, 2½" x 21" (you will use 31)
	8 strips, 2½" x 42"	
	10 strips, 2¼" x 42"	
Dark blue print	9 strips, 6½" x 42"	

This quilt has two different colorations of the simple Nine Patch block that alternate with plain squares. Don't you just love the versatile Nine Patch? I would never have guessed I had such a large collection of pastels. Try to use 35 different strips, 2½" x 42". Shop for what you don't have or swap with your friends if necessary.

Making Block A

After sewing each seam, press the seam allowances in the direction indicated by the arrows.

1. Sew three pastel strips together along the long edges to make a strip set. Repeat to make a total of 19 strip sets, joining different prints in each set. Press the seam allowances in either direction. Crosscut the strip sets into 140 segments, 2½" wide.

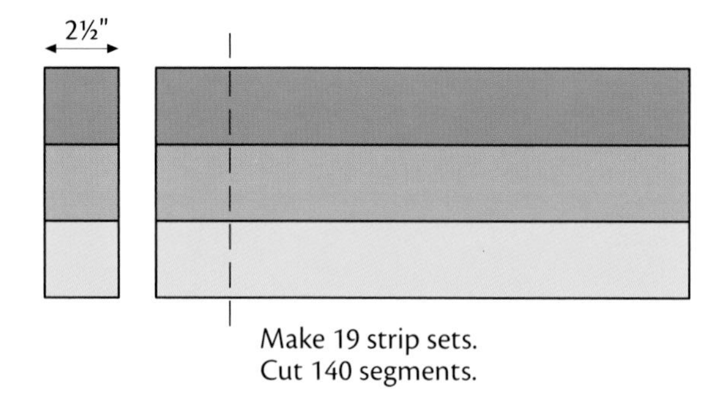

Make 19 strip sets.
Cut 140 segments.

2. Sew three pastel segments together to make block A, rotating the segments or re-pressing the seam allowances so they alternate. Make 30 blocks. Set aside the remaining 50 segments for the pieced third border.

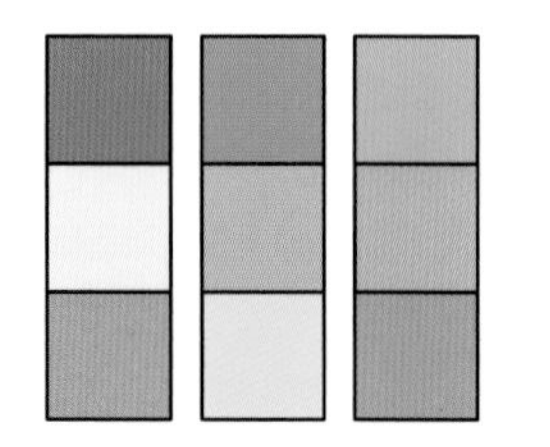

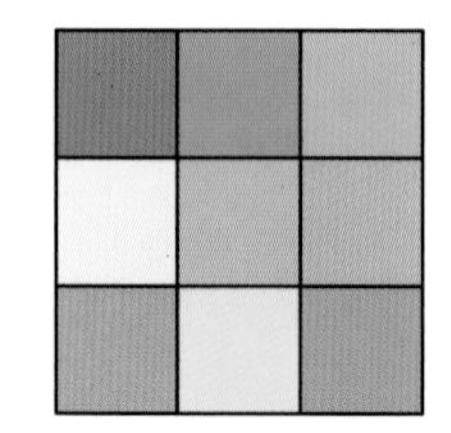

Block A.
Make 30.

Making Block B and the Border Block

1. Using the 2½" x 21" strips, sew a dark blue tone-on-tone fabric strip to each long edge of a pastel strip to make a strip set. Make 15 strip sets. Crosscut the strip sets into 120 segments, 2½" wide.

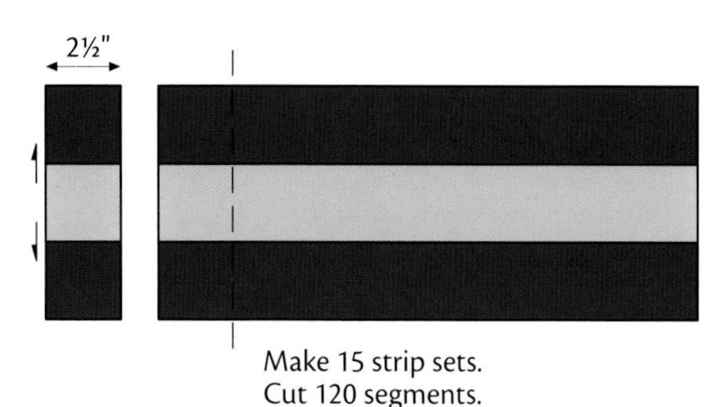

Make 15 strip sets.
Cut 120 segments.

2. Using the 2½" x 42" strips, sew a cream strip to each long edge of a dark blue tone-on-tone fabric strip to make a strip set. Make four strip sets. Make a half strip set in the same manner using the 2½" x 21" dark blue and cream strips. Crosscut the strip sets into 71 segments, 2½" wide.

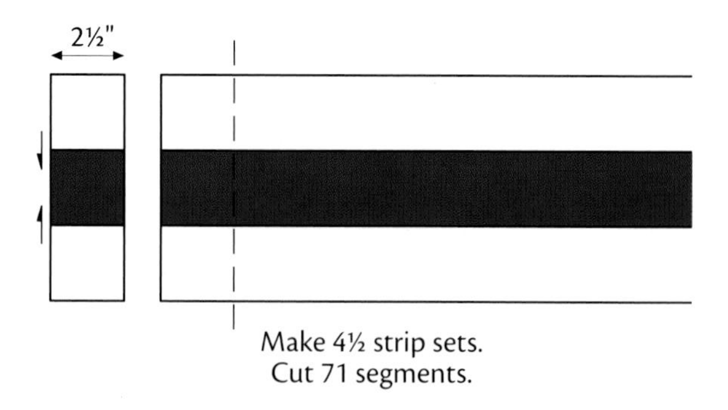

Make 4½ strip sets.
Cut 71 segments.

3. Sew segments from steps 1 and 2 together as shown to make 49 of block B and 22 border blocks.

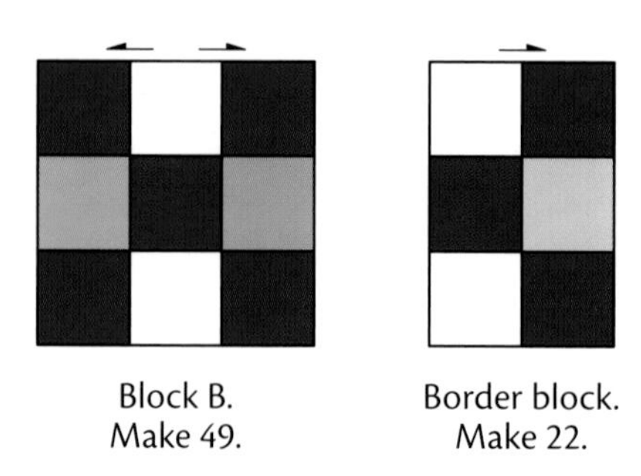

Block B.
Make 49.

Border block.
Make 22.

Assembling the Quilt Top

1. Alternately sew together five of block A and four of block B. Add a border block to each end of the row as shown to complete row 1. Make six rows.

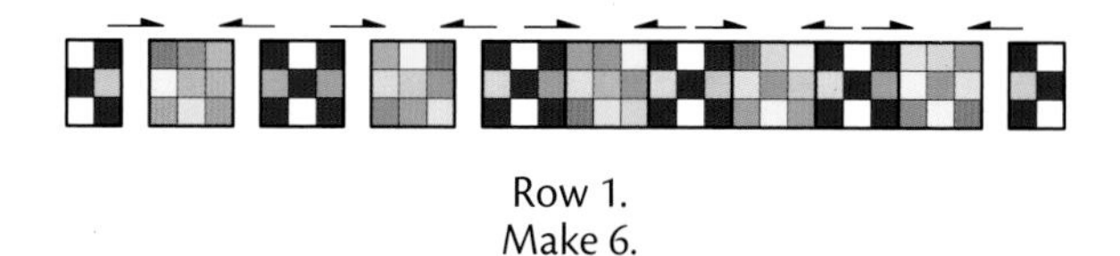

Row 1.
Make 6.

2. Alternately sew together five of block B and four 6½" cream squares. Add a 4½" x 6½" cream rectangle to each end of the row to complete row 2. Make five rows.

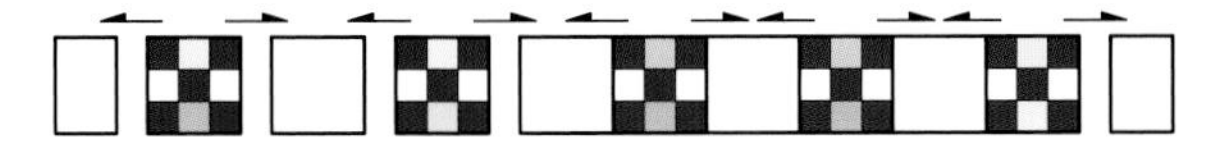

Row 2.
Make 5.

3. Alternately join five border blocks and four 4½" x 6½" cream rectangles. Add a 4½" cream square to each end of the row to complete the top pieced border row. Repeat to make the bottom pieced border row.

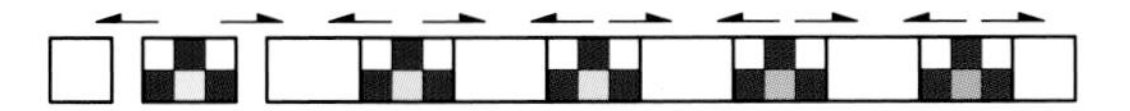

Top/bottom border row.
Make 2.

4. Alternately lay out rows 1 and 2, arranging them as necessary to distribute the color well. Sew the rows together. Attach the top and bottom pieced border rows.
5. Attach the 2½"-wide dark blue border strips to the quilt top, referring to "Adding Borders" on page 15 to measure, cut, and sew them. Add the borders to the sides first, and then the top and bottom edges.
6. Using the pastel strip-set segments you set aside earlier, join 13 segments end to end to make a side border. Make two pieced borders. Sew these borders to the sides of the quilt top. Join 12 segments end to end to make the top pieced border. Remove one square from the strip. Repeat to make the bottom pieced border. Sew these borders to the top and bottom of the quilt top.

Top/bottom border.
Make 2.

Side border.
Make 2.

7. Repeat step 5 to attach the 6½"-wide dark blue print fourth-border strips to the quilt.

Quilt assembly

Finishing the Quilt

Refer to "Finishing Techniques" on page 16 for detailed instructions.

1. Layer the quilt top with the batting and backing; baste.
2. Hand or machine quilt. Follow the quilting suggestions shown below or use your own design.

Quilting diagram

3. Use the 2¼"-wide dark blue tone-on-tone strips to bind the edges of your quilt.

Make **Momma** Happy

Pieced and quilted by Gayle Bong

Finished quilt: 48½" x 64½"

Finished block: 16"

Materials

Yardages are based on 42"-wide fabric.

12 fat quarters of assorted bright prints for block backgrounds

12 fat eighths of assorted contrasting bright prints for block spools

½ yard of fabric for binding

3¼ yards of fabric for backing

54" x 70" piece of batting

Mom loved these fabrics when she saw them at my house. I ran with her hint and surprised her with this quilt. It sure was fun using these funky prints and thinking of mom. Choose 12 fat quarters for block backgrounds and 12 fat eighths for the spools. Vary the size of the prints in each block using a contrasting color rather than a contrasting value.

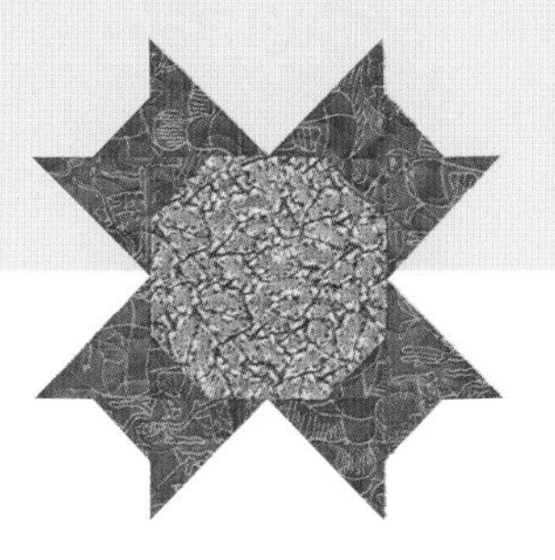

Cutting		
Please read all the instructions before starting.		
FABRIC	FIRST CUT	FOLLOWING CUT(S)
Fat quarters	2 strips *each,* 4½" x 21" (24 total)	8 squares *each,* 4½" x 4½" (96 total)
	1 strip *each,* 4⅞" x 21" (12 total)	4 squares *each,* 4⅞" x 4⅞"; cut *each* square in half diagonally to make 8 triangles (96 total)
Fat eighths	1 strip *each,* 4⅞" x 21" (12 total)	4 squares *each,* 4⅞" x 4⅞"; cut *each* square in half diagonally to make 8 triangles (96 total)
	1 strip *each,* 2½" x 21" (12 total)	8 squares *each,* 2½" x 2½" (96 total)
Binding fabric	6 strips, 2¼" x 21"	

Making the Blocks

Keep matching fabrics together so pieces from one fat quarter and one fat eighth are used in each block. After sewing each seam, press the seam allowances in the direction indicated by the arrows.

1. Draw a diagonal line from corner to corner on the wrong side of each 2½" square. Place a 2½" square on top of a fat quarter 4½" square. With right sides together and edges matched, stitch on the drawn line. Trim the seam allowances to ¼"; press. Make eight units.

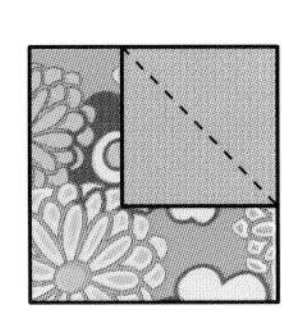

Make 8.

2. Sew a fat-eighth and a fat-quarter triangle together. Make eight half-square-triangle units.

Make 8.

3. Sew two units from step 1 and two units from step 2 together as shown to make a spool unit. Make four units. Sew the units together as shown.

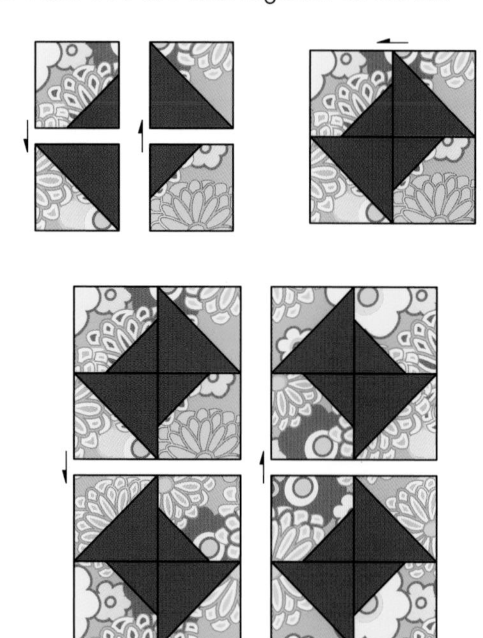

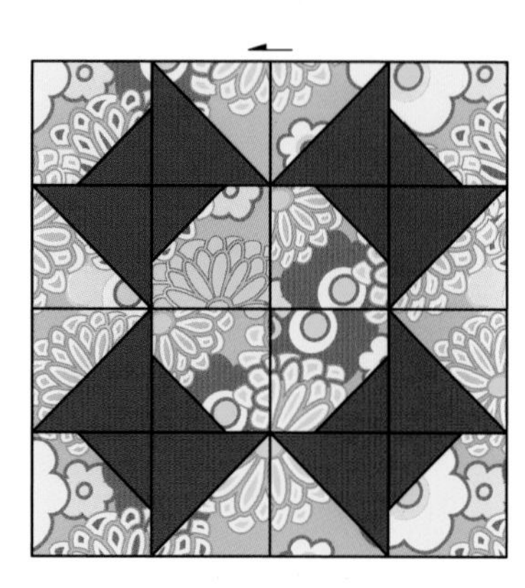

4. Repeat steps 1–3 to make a total of 12 Spinning Spools blocks.

Assembling the Quilt Top

1. Arrange the blocks to your liking in four rows of three blocks each. Sew the blocks into rows, and then sew the rows together.

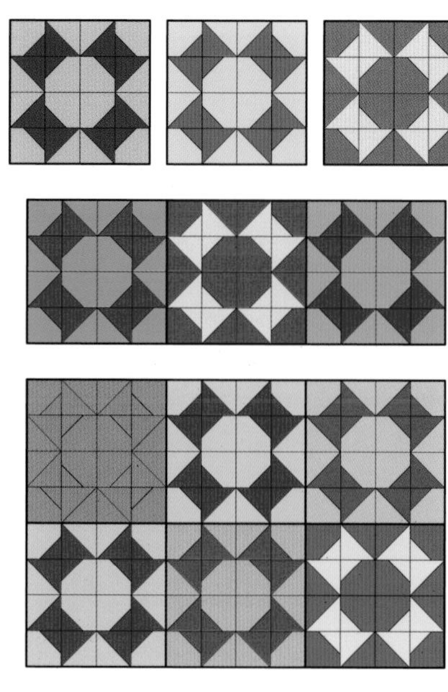

Quilt assembly

2. Stay stitch ⅛" from the edge of the quilt top. This will prevent the seams in the blocks from coming loose around the edge of the quilt.

Finishing the Quilt

Refer to "Finishing Techniques" on page 16 for detailed instructions.

1. Layer the quilt top with the batting and backing; baste.
2. Hand or machine quilt. I used my long-arm quilting machine to quilt a pantograph (a design that goes from one edge to the other with no breaks) I found on the Internet.
3. Use the 2¼"-wide strips to bind the edges of your quilt.

Twin Peaks **Towers**

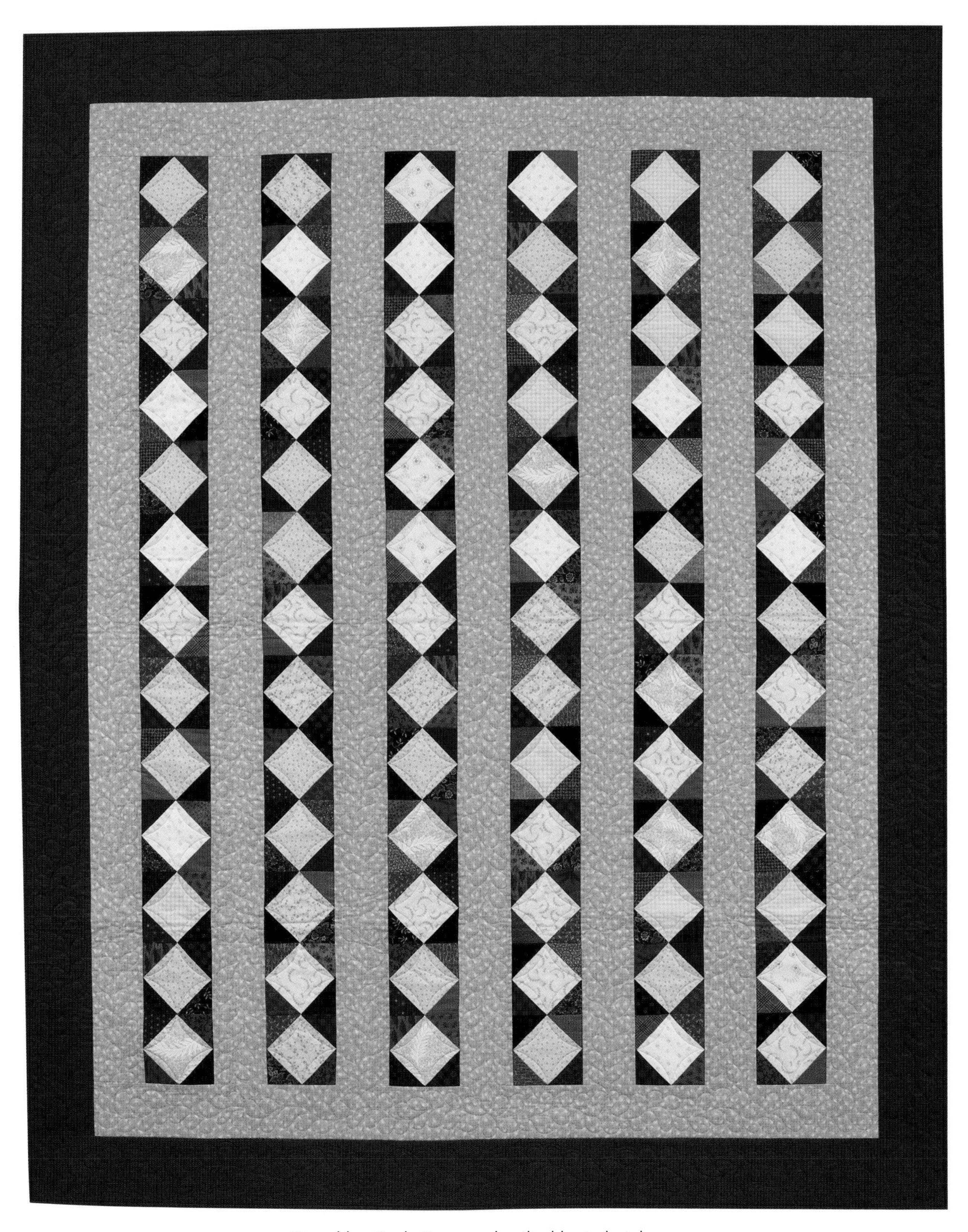

Pieced by Gayle Bong and quilted by Judy Johnson

I have fallen in love with strippy quilts. This is made with a fun technique I call Twin Peaks. You'll need to cut 30 strips, 3½" x 21", of medium and dark prints. Be sure none of the colors clash or you will spot it instantly with its mate, and it will be obvious that this quilt was strip pieced.

Finished quilt: 70" x 86¾"

Materials

Yardages are based on 42"-wide fabric.

2 yards of cream fabric for sashing and inner border

2 yards of green fabric for outer border and binding

1¾ yards *total* of assorted medium and dark scraps for pieced strips

1¼ yards *total* of assorted cream fabrics for pieced strips

5¾ yards of fabric for backing

76" x 93" piece of batting

Cutting

Please read all the instructions before starting.

FABRIC	FIRST CUT	FOLLOWING CUT
Assorted medium and dark scraps	30 strips, 3½" x 21"	
	15 squares, 3½" x 3½"	Cut each square in half diagonally to make 30 triangles
Assorted creams	9 strips, 4¼" x 42"	78 squares, 4¼" x 4¼"
Cream (sashing/ inner border)	9 *lengthwise-cut* strips, 4½" x 72"	
Green	8 strips, 5½" x 42"	
	8 strips, 2¼" x 42"	

Making the Rows

After sewing each seam, press the seam allowances in the direction indicated by the arrows.

1. Place two 3½"-wide medium and/or dark strips right sides together, staggering the ends at the beginning 11" to 12". Cut off the staggered portion of the strip and set it aside. Sew the strips together along one long edge. When you reach the end of the top or bottom strip, simply butt another strip up to it. Just make sure you position the strips so right sides are together. Sew all the strips into one long strip set using the portion you cut off from the staggered beginning of the strip at the end of the strip set. Then sew along the opposite long edge to form a tube. Press the strip set to set the seams. Crosscut the strip set into 72 squares, 3½" wide, trimming off any segment where strips were butted. Cut each square in half diagonally, alternating the direction of *each*

diagonal cut, to make 144 Twin Peak units. Press *all* the seam allowances in the same direction.

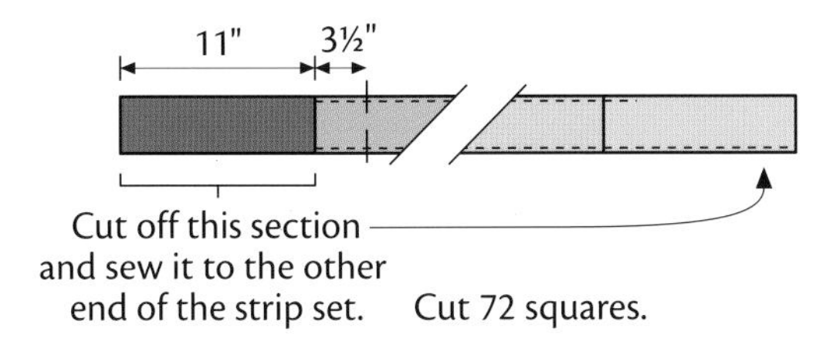

Cut off this section and sew it to the other end of the strip set. Cut 72 squares.

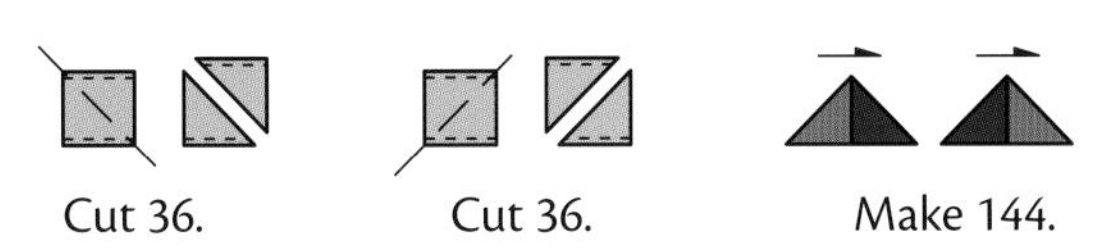
Cut 36. Cut 36. Make 144.

2. Sew Twin Peaks units to opposite sides of a cream square. Make 66 parallelogram units.

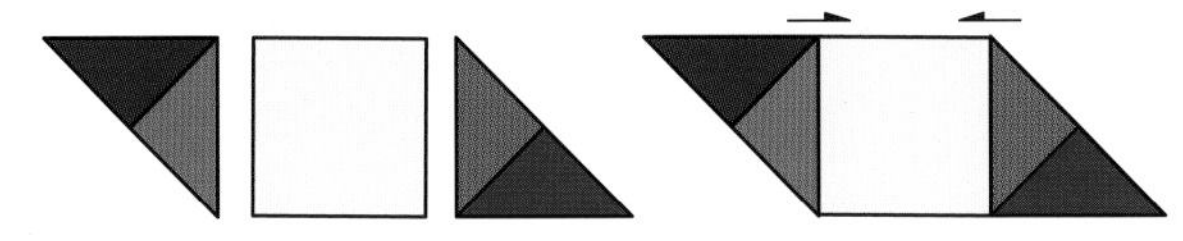
Make 66.

3. Sew together one cream square, one Twin Peaks unit, and two different medium or dark triangles as shown to make a row end unit. Make 12 end units. You will use 24 medium/dark triangles. The six extra were cut for variety and can be added to your scrap box.

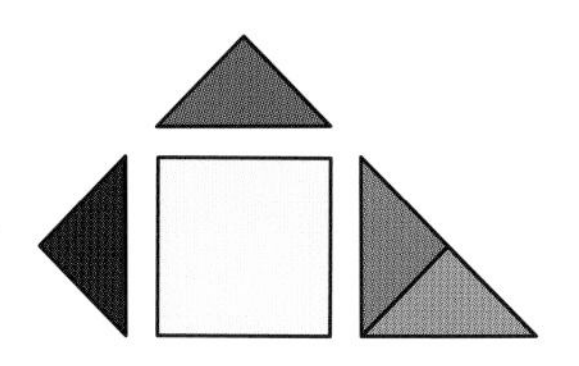
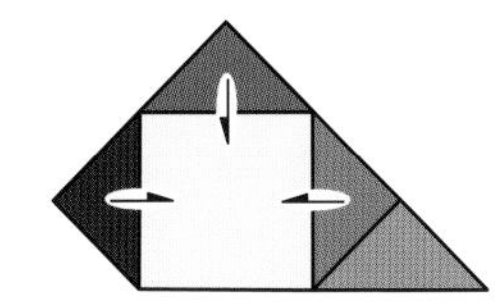
Make 12.

4. Sew 11 parallelogram units together to make a row. Stitch an end unit to each end of the row; press. Make six rows.

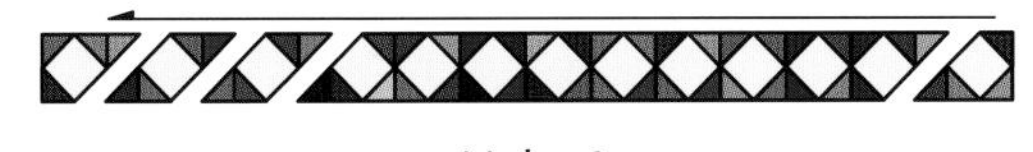
Make 6.

Assembling the Quilt Top

1. Measure the length of each of the six rows. (Mathematically, if you stitched perfectly they should measure 68¾".) If the strip measurements differ, calculate the average. Trim seven of the 4½" x 72" cream strips to the length determined. Pin mark the center and quarter points of each row and each strip.
2. Alternately arrange the cream strips and block rows vertically. Sew the block rows and strips together, matching pins and ends. Take extra care to be sure the blocks align horizontally from row to row.
3. Attach the remaining two cream strips to the quilt top and bottom edges, referring to "Adding Borders" on page 15 to measure, cut, and sew them.
4. Attach the 5½"-wide green outer-border strips to the quilt top, referring to "Adding Borders" to measure, cut, and sew them.

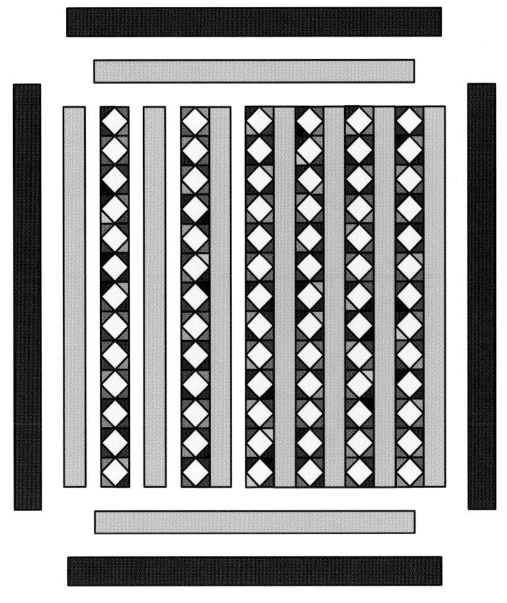
Quilt assembly

Finishing the Quilt

Refer to "Finishing Techniques" on page 16 for detailed instructions.

1. Layer the quilt top with the batting and backing; baste.
2. Hand or machine quilt. Follow the quilting suggestions shown below or use your own design.

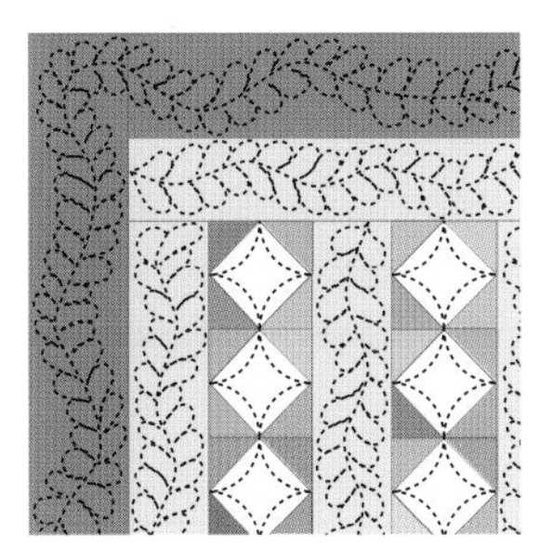
Quilting diagram

3. Use the 2¼"-wide green strips to bind the edges of your quilt.

Midnight **Express**

Pieced and quilted by Gayle Bong

Finished quilt: 72" x 72"

Finished block: 8½"

Materials

Yardages are based on 42"-wide fabric.

2⅔ yards *total* of assorted black fabrics for blocks

1¾ yards of black print for borders and binding

1½ yards *total* of assorted pastel prints for blocks and pieced border

1⅛ yards of medium-light grayish green fabric for blocks

4½ yards of fabric for backing

80" x 80" piece of batting

Cutting

Please read all the instructions before starting.

FABRIC	FIRST CUT	FOLLOWING CUT
Assorted pastel prints	24 sets of 4 matching squares, 3½" x 3½" (96 total)	
	2½"-wide strips in random lengths (you will need the equivalent of 20 strips, 2½" x 14")	
Grayish green	5 strips, 7" x 42"	25 squares, 7" x 7"
Assorted blacks	24 sets of matching pieces consisting of: 1 square, 3½" x 3½" (24 total)	
	2 squares, 3" x 3" (48 total)	Cut each 3" square in half diagonally to make 4 triangles (96 total)
	1 square, 5½" x 5½" (24 total)	Cut each 5½" square into quarters diagonally to make 4 triangles (96 total)
	25 sets of matching pieces consisting of: 2 rectangles, 1½" x 7" (50 total) 2 rectangles, 1½" x 9" (50 total)	
Black print	4 squares, 5½" x 5½"	
	7 strips, 1½" x 42"	
	7 strips, 3½" x 42"	
	8 strips, 2¼" x 42"	

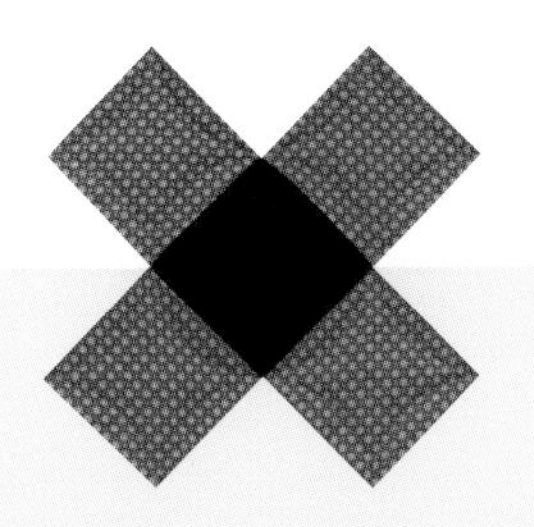

Some piles of fabric sit around so long that eventually they end up next to each other and become friends, at least in my studio! Keep the large squares a medium-light color to showcase your quilting, or feature a novelty print in them. If you choose a novelty print, it's especially important to have a contrasting fabric frame the squares. Gather 24 sets of four matching squares, each 3½" x 3½", for the pieced blocks.

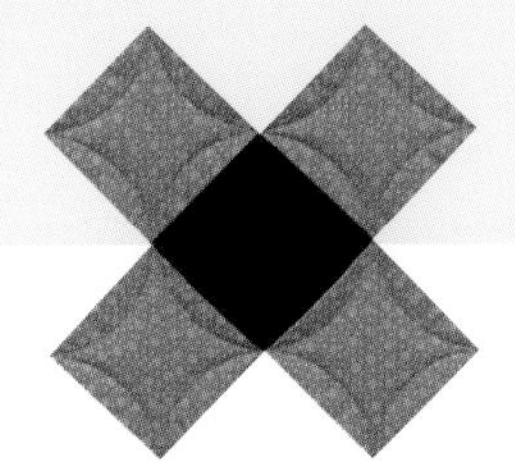

Making the Criss Cross Blocks

Arrange four matching pastel squares, one black 3½" square, four black 3" triangles, and four black 5½" triangles in diagonal rows as shown. Sew the pieces in each row together. Press the seam allowances toward the black. Sew the rows together. Press the seam allowances away from the center. Make 24 Criss Cross blocks.

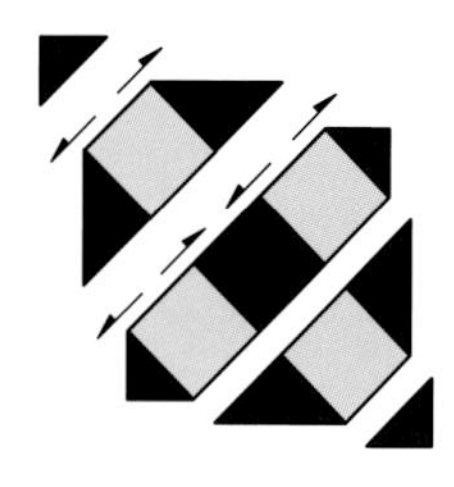

Criss Cross block.
Make 24.

Making the Framed Square Blocks

Using one set of matching black rectangles, sew the 1½" x 7" rectangles to opposite sides of a grayish green square; press. Sew the black 1½" x 9" rectangles to the remaining sides of the square. Make 25 Framed Square blocks.

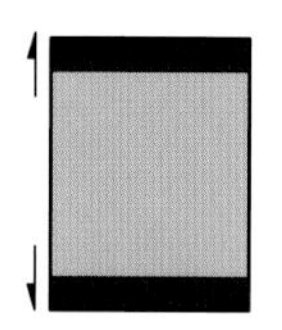
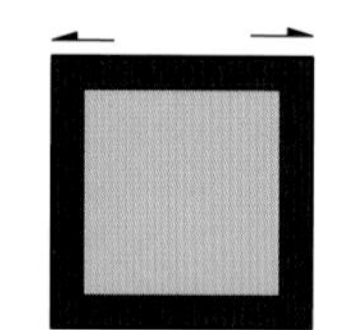

Framed Square block.
Make 25.

Assembling the Quilt Top

1. Refer to the quilt assembly diagram to arrange the blocks in seven rows of seven blocks each, alternating the Criss Cross blocks with the Framed Square blocks as shown. Play with the position of the blocks until you're pleased with the color arrangement. Sew the blocks into rows, pressing the seam allowances toward the Framed Square blocks. Sew the rows together; press.
2. Attach the black 1½"-wide inner-border strips to the quilt top, referring to "Adding Borders" on page 15 to measure, cut, and sew them.
3. The quilt top should measure 62" x 62". Measure the length and width of your quilt top and adjust the following borders accordingly. Sew the pastel 2½"-wide random-length strips together end to end to make four border strips the length measured. Sew black print 3½"-wide strips together to make four border strips the length measured. Sew each pastel border to a black border. Sew the pastel edge of a border strip to opposite sides of the quilt top. Sew a black 5½" square to each end of the remaining two borders, and then sew them to the quilt top.

Make 2 of each.

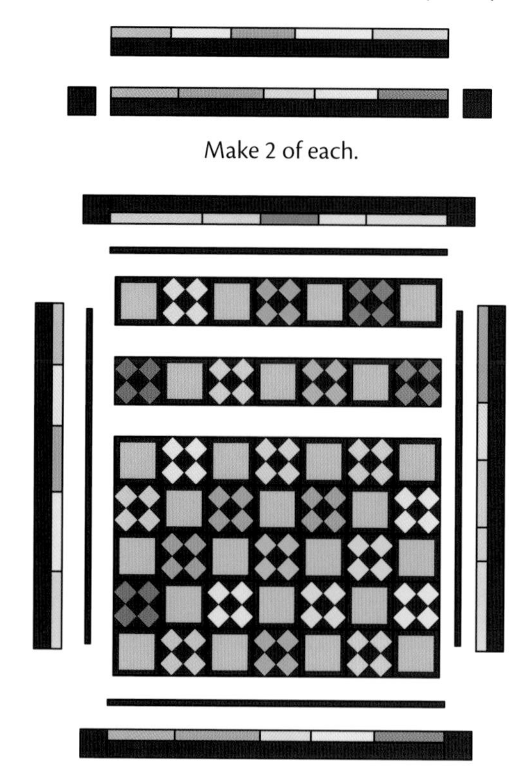

Quilt assembly

Finishing the Quilt

Refer to "Finishing Techniques" on page 16 for detailed instructions.

1. Layer the quilt top with the batting and backing; baste.
2. Hand or machine quilt. Follow the quilting suggestions shown below or use your own design.

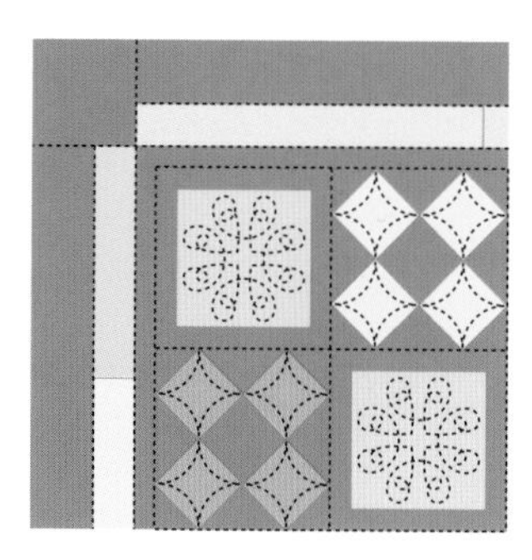

Quilting diagram

3. Use the black 2¼"-wide strips to bind the edges of your quilt.

Challenge No. 174

Pieced and quilted by Gayle Bong

Finished quilt: 56½" x 56½"

Finished block: 8"

Materials

Yardages are based on 42"-wide fabric.

1⅝ yards *total* of assorted light scraps for blocks and middle border

1⅛ yards *total* of assorted medium and dark scraps for blocks and middle border

1 yard of dark blue fabric for outer border and binding

⅝ yard of light blue fabric for inner border

⅝ yard of medium blue fabric for inner border

3⅞ yards of fabric for backing

62" x 62" piece of batting

The name refers to the number assigned to the Fox and Geese block in the book my guild used when choosing the block for a challenge. This quilt is the perfect place for the little light and dark scraps that you cut into 2" finished squares and half-square triangles. Choose the two border fabrics first so you can coordinate the scraps.

Cutting		
Please read all the instructions before starting.		
FABRIC	FIRST CUT	FOLLOWING CUT
Assorted light scraps	132 squares, 2½" x 2½"	
	124 squares, 2⅞" x 2⅞"*	Cut each square in half diagonally to make 248 triangles
Assorted medium and dark scraps	40 squares, 2½" x 2½"	
	124 squares, 2⅞" x 2⅞"*	Cut each square in half diagonally to make 248 triangles
Light blue	4 strips, 4½" x 32½"	
Medium blue	4 strips, 4½" x 32½"	
Dark blue	6 strips, 2½" x 42"	
	6 strips, 2¼" x 42"	
**Refer to "Cutting Triangles Using a Triangle-Cutting Ruler" on page 13 for an alternate way to cut triangles from 2½" strips.*		

Making the Blocks

After sewing each seam, press the seam allowances in the direction indicated by the arrows.

1. Sew together one light triangle and one dark triangle to make a half-square-triangle unit. Repeat to make a total of 248 units. Set aside 96 units for the border.

Make 248.

Pairing Colors

Although the design requires light and dark scraps, invariably medium-toned scraps will get in the mix. To make the best use of your scraps, always pair two triangles with the greatest contrast (refer to "Contrast" on page 9).

2. Sew a half-square-triangle unit from step 1 to a light 2½" square. Make 72 units. Stitch two of these units together as shown. Repeat to make a total of 36.

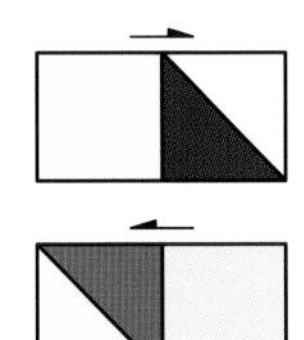
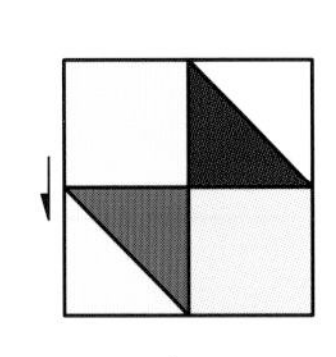

Make 36.

3. Sew a half-square-triangle unit each to one light and one dark 2½" square. Sew these units together as shown. Make 40 units.

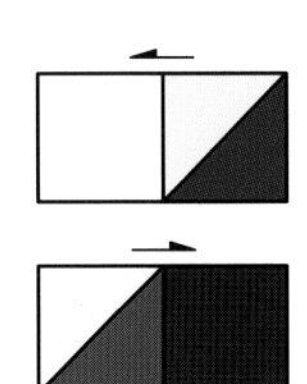
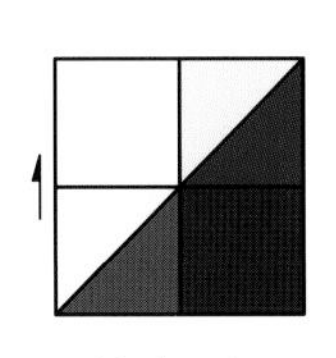

Make 40.

4. Sew two units from step 2 and two units from step 3 together to make a Fox and Geese block. Make 16 blocks.

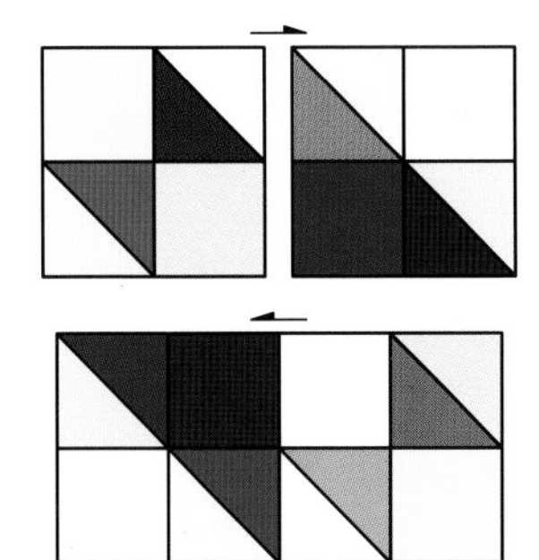
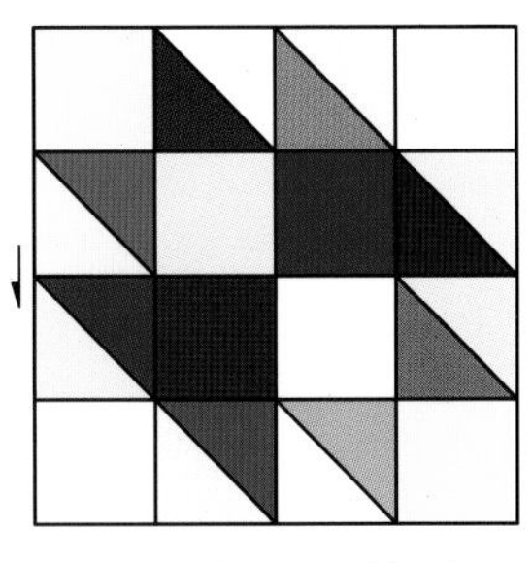

Fox and Geese block.
Make 16.

5. Sew together four light 2½" squares as shown. Make four four-patch units.

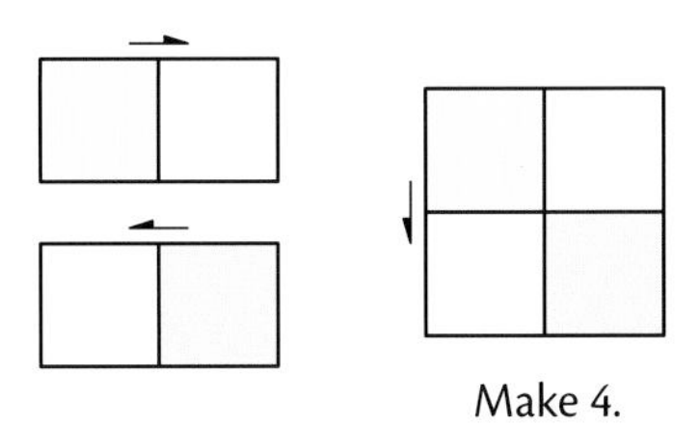

Make 4.

6. Sew one unit from step 2, two units from step 3, and one four-patch unit from step 5 together to make a Modified Fox and Geese block. Make four blocks.

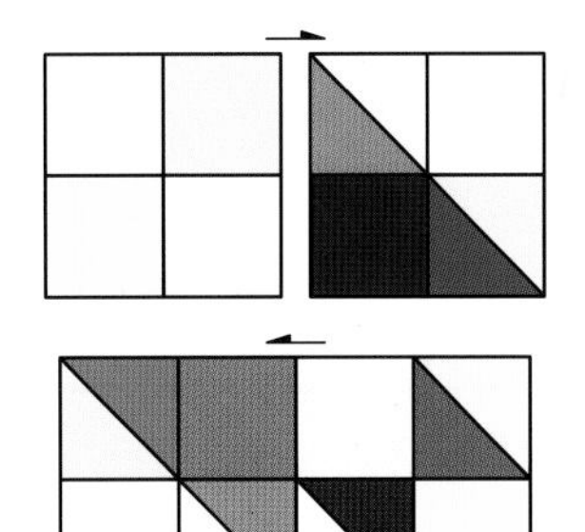
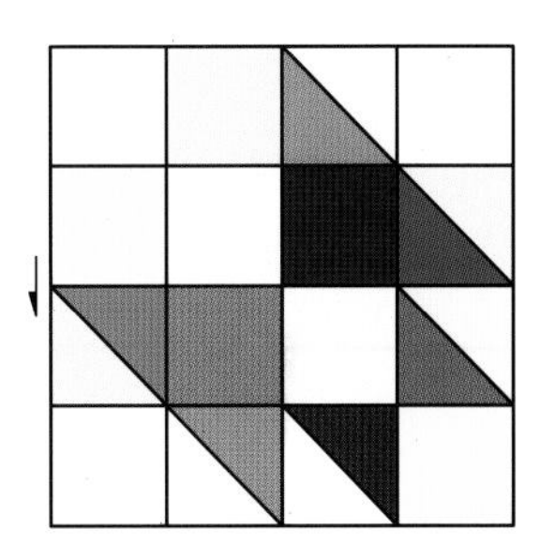

Modified Fox and Geese block.
Make 4.

Assembling the Quilt Top

1. Arrange 12 Fox and Geese blocks around the four Modified Fox and Geese blocks as shown. Sew the blocks into rows, and then sew the rows together.

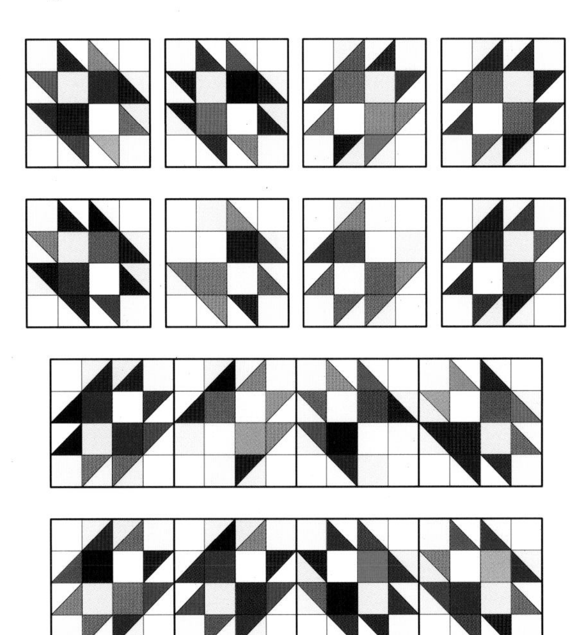

2. Sew each light blue strip to a medium blue strip along one long edge to make four border strips, 32½" long. Refer to the quilt assembly diagram at right to sew two of the borders to the sides of the quilt top. Sew one of the remaining Fox and Geese blocks to each end of the remaining two border strips as shown. Sew these borders to the top and bottom edges of the quilt top.

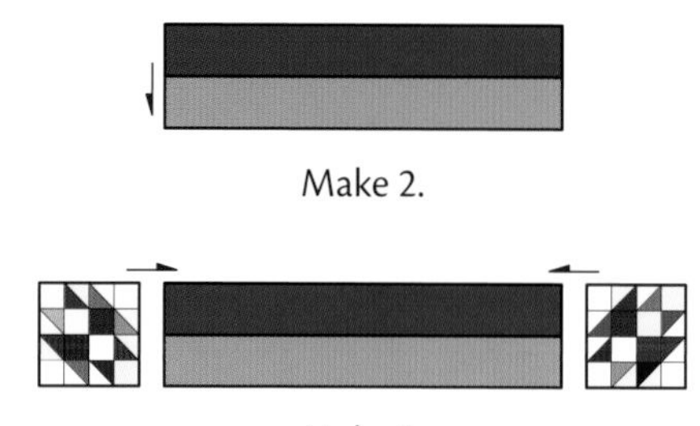

Make 2.

Make 2.

3. Join 24 half-square-triangle units as shown, with half of the dark triangles facing one direction and the other half facing the opposite direction. Make four border units. Sew two of the borders to the sides of the quilt top with the dark-triangle side against the medium-blue borders. Add light 2½" squares to opposite ends of the remaining two borders and sew them to the top and bottom edges of the quilt top.

Side border.
Make 2.

Top/bottom border.
Make 2.

4. Attach the dark blue 2½"-wide outer-border strips to the quilt top, referring to "Adding Borders" on page 15 to measure, cut, and sew them.

Quilt assembly

Finishing the Quilt

Refer to "Finishing Techniques" on page 16 for detailed instructions.

1. Layer the quilt top with the batting and backing; baste.
2. Hand or machine quilt. Follow the quilting suggestions shown below or use your own design.

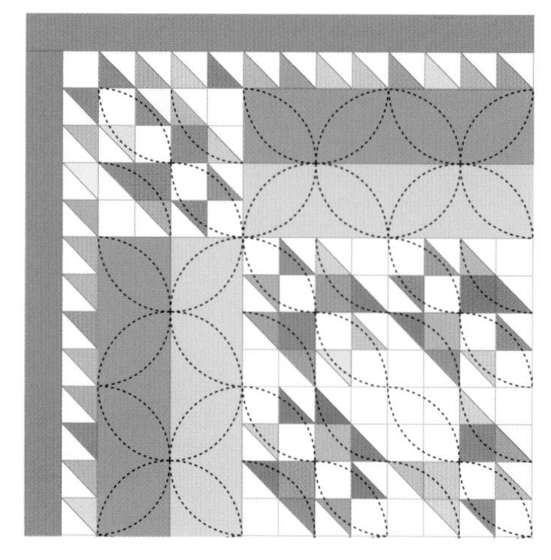

Quilting diagram

3. Use the dark blue 2¼"-wide strips to bind the edges of your quilt.

Box Boy

Pieced and quilted by Gayle Bong

Finished quilt: 62½" x 70"

Finished block: 7½"

This variation of the Friendship Star block has pairs of trapezoids that add a little interest to an otherwise simple block. Cutting is easy with a triangle-cutting ruler. The cream stars could be one print or many prints positioned the same within each star or randomly placed. Don't hesitate to swap or shop for the 56 medium and dark strips, 1¾" x 42".

Materials

Yardage is based on 42"-wide fabric.

3¼ yards *total* of assorted medium and dark scraps for blocks

1¾ yards *total* of assorted cream scraps for blocks

1⅔ yards of red fabric for border and binding

4 yards of fabric for backing

70" x 76" piece of batting

Half-square triangle-cutting ruler (refer to "Cutting Triangles" on page 12)

Cutting

Please read all the instructions before starting.

FABRIC	FIRST CUT	FOLLOWING CUT
Assorted medium and dark scraps	56 strips, 1¾" x 42"	Crosscut *each* strip in half to make 112 strips, 1¾" x 21"
Assorted cream scraps	56 strips, 3" x 11"	1 square, 3" x 3", from *each* strip (56 total)
		4 triangles from *each* strip (224 total)*
Red	7 strips, 5¼" x 42"	
	7 strips, 2¼" x 42"	

**Refer to "Cutting Triangles Using a Triangle-Cutting Ruler" on page 13 for instructions to cut triangles using a half-square triangle-cutting ruler.*

Making the Blocks

Keep matching cream pieces together for each block as I did or mix them up. After sewing each seam, press the seam allowances in the direction indicated by the arrows.

1. Sew one medium and one dark 1¾"-wide strip together along the long edges to make a strip set. Press the seam allowances in either direction. Make 56 strip sets. Use the triangle-cutting ruler to measure and cut a 5⅞"-wide trapezoid from one strip. For the next cut, rotate the triangle ruler and align the angled cut edge of

the strip set with the angle of the triangle-cutting ruler. Cut four trapezoids from each strip set for a total of 224 trapezoids.

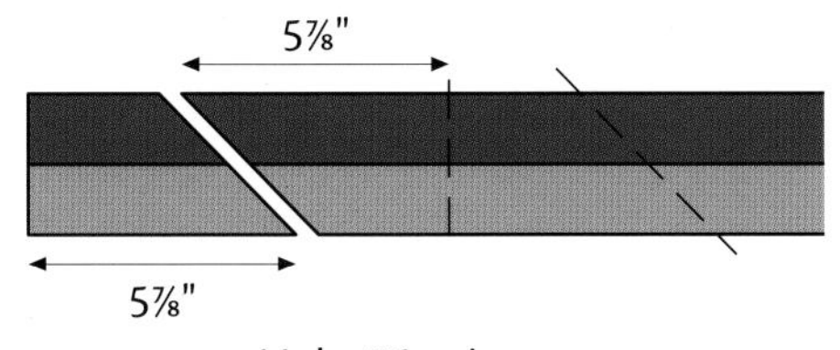

Make 56 strip sets.
Cut 224 trapezoids.

Out of Orbit

Cut all the trapezoids facing the same direction or some stars will be spinning off on their own path.

Right Wrong

2. Sew a cream triangle to each trapezoid.

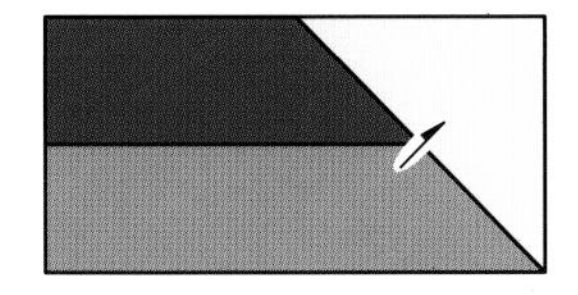

3. Arrange four trapezoid units and a cream 3" square as shown. Sew the left-hand trapezoid unit to the square first, leaving about 1½" of the square open at the end of the seam. Working in a counterclockwise direction around the cream center square, sew a trapezoid unit to each edge of the square. After the last unit is added, sew the small open section of the first unit to the square to complete the block. Make 56 blocks.

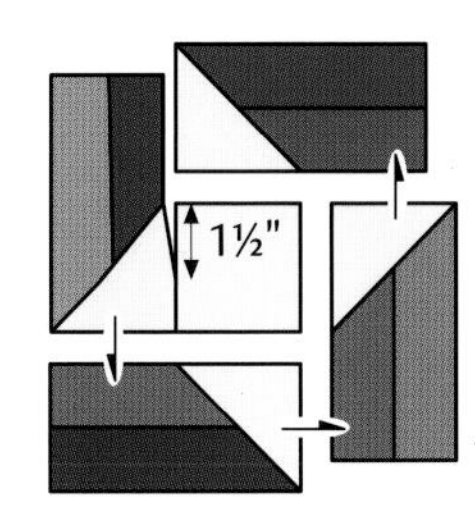

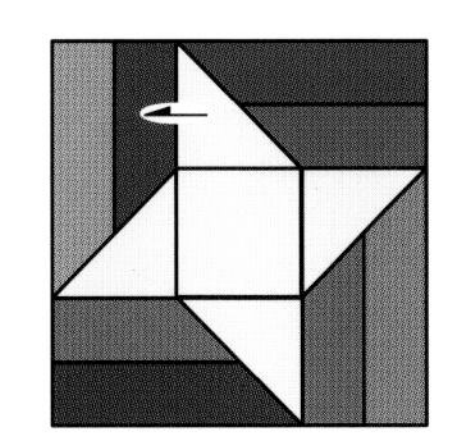

Make 56.

Assembling the Quilt Top

1. Arrange the blocks in eight rows of seven blocks each. When you're happy with the color arrangement, sew the blocks into rows, and then sew the rows together.
2. Attach the red 5¼"-wide strips to the quilt top, referring to "Adding Borders" on page 15 to measure, cut, and sew them.

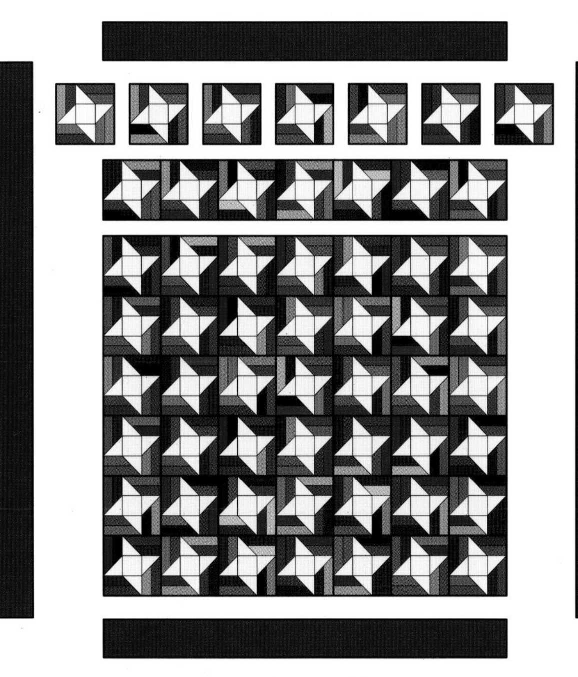

Quilt assembly

Finishing the Quilt

Refer to "Finishing Techniques" on page 16 for detailed instructions.

1. Layer the quilt top with the batting and backing; baste.
2. Hand or machine quilt. I chose a pantograph (a design that goes from one edge to the other with no breaks) I found on the Internet to quilt using my long-arm quilting machine.
3. Use the red 2¼"-wide strips to bind the edges of your quilt.

Patchwork Park

Pieced and quilted by Gayle Bong

When I'm in the mood to sew, I'm glad I have my scraps already cut. This quilt is one of several in the book that required little preliminary cutting because I keep my scraps organized. Light to dark 3" finished squares and triangles were put to good use here. Cut your darkest scraps into triangles for both blocks. Use your medium and dark fabrics for squares in the Contrary Wife blocks. Select 13 gold or tan squares for the center of the Album blocks.

Finished quilt: 60" x 60"

Finished block: 9"

Materials

Yardages are based on 42"-wide fabric.

2½ yards *total* of assorted medium and dark scraps for blocks and inner border

1½ yards of dark blue fabric for outer border and binding

1⅓ yards *total* of assorted light scraps for blocks and inner border

¼ yard *total* of assorted medium gold and medium tan scraps for Album blocks

4 yards of fabric for backing

66" x 66" piece of batting

Cutting		
Please read all the instructions before starting.		
FABRIC	FIRST CUT	FOLLOWING CUT
Assorted light scraps	38 squares, 3⅞" x 3⅞"*	Cut each square in half diagonally to make 76 large half-square triangles
	8 squares 3½" x 3½"	
	52 squares, 2⅜" x 2⅜"*	Cut each square in half diagonally to make 104 small half-square triangles
Assorted medium and dark scraps	52 squares, 2" x 2"	
	140 squares, 3½" x 3½"	
	64 squares, 3⅞" x 3⅞"*	Cut each square in half diagonally to make128 large half-square triangles
Assorted medium gold and medium tan scraps	13 squares, 3½" x 3½"	
Dark blue	6 strips, 4¾" x 42"	
	7 strips, 2¼" x 42"	
**Refer to "Cutting Triangles Using a Triangle-Cutting Ruler" on page 13 for an alternate way to cut the triangles from strips.*		

Making the Album Blocks

After sewing each seam, press the seam allowances in the direction indicated by the arrows.

1. Sew small light triangles to adjacent sides of a dark 2" square. Make 52 units.

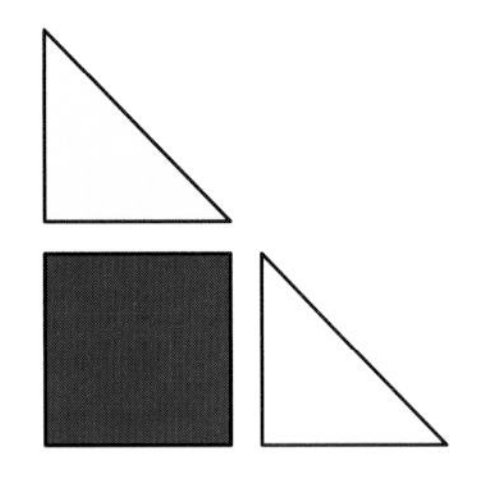
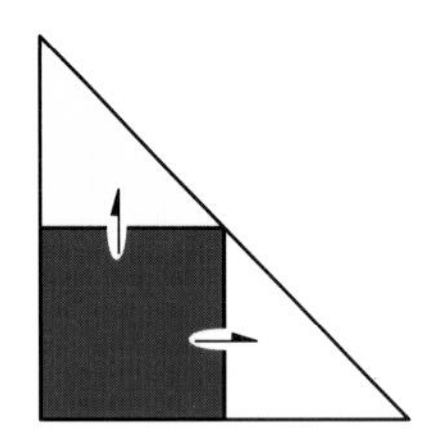

Make 52.

2. Sew a dark 3⅞" triangle to each unit from step 1. Make 52 units.

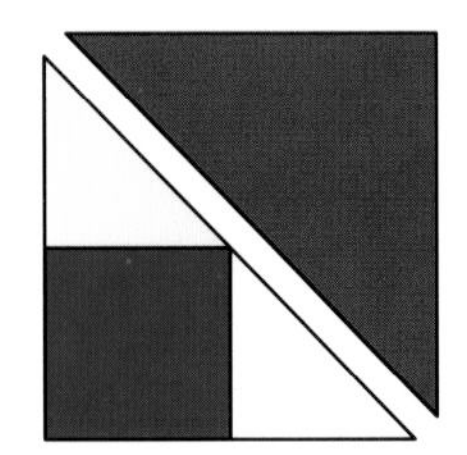
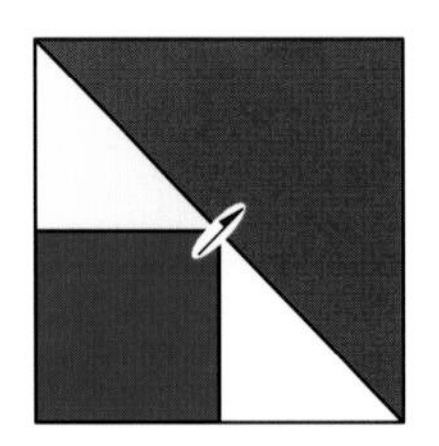

Make 52.

3. Arrange four dark 3½" squares, one tan or gold square, and four units from step 2 as shown. Sew the pieces into rows, and then sew the rows together. Make 13 Album blocks.

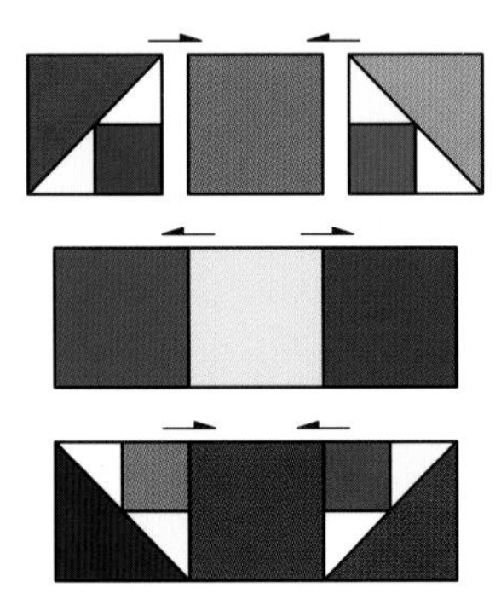
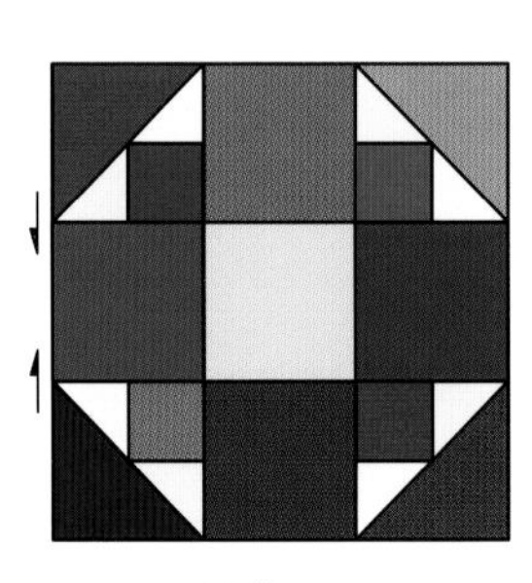

Make 13.

Making the Contrary Wife Blocks

1. Sew a light triangle to a dark triangle to make a half-square-triangle unit. Make 76 units. Set aside 16 units for the inner border.

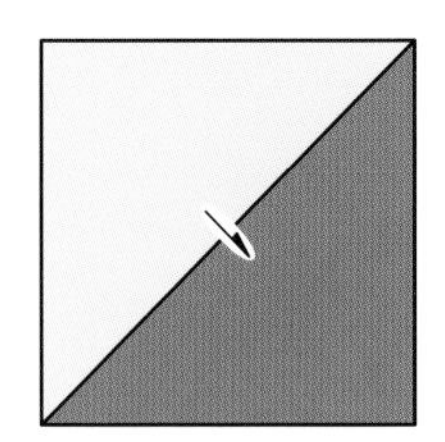

Make 76.

2. Sew dark 3½" squares to opposite sides of a half-square-triangle unit. Make 36 rows.

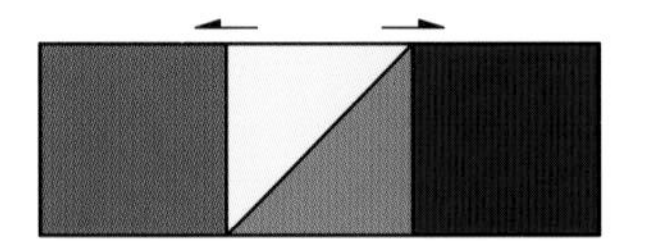

Make 36.

3. Sew a half-square-triangle unit to opposite sides of a dark 3½" square. Make 12 rows.

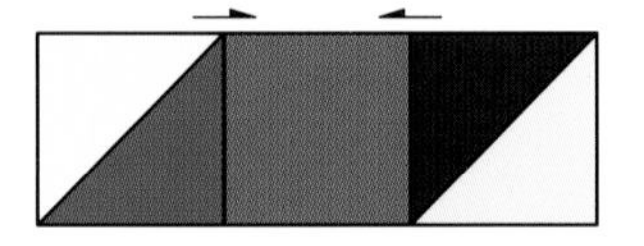

Make 12.

4. Sew two rows from step 2 and one row from step 3 together as shown to make a Contrary Wife block. Make 12 blocks. Set aside the remaining rows from step 2 for the inner border.

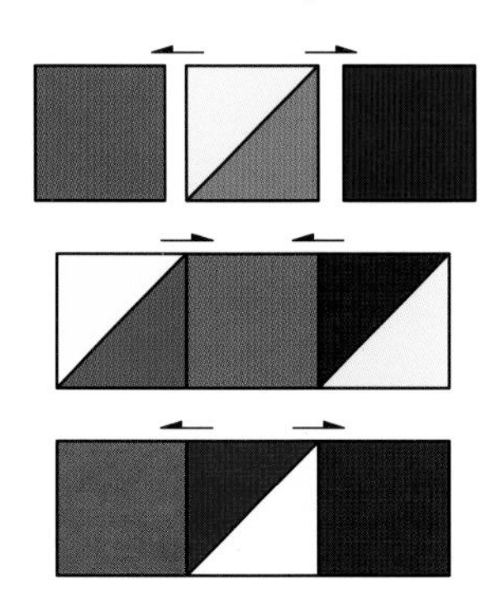
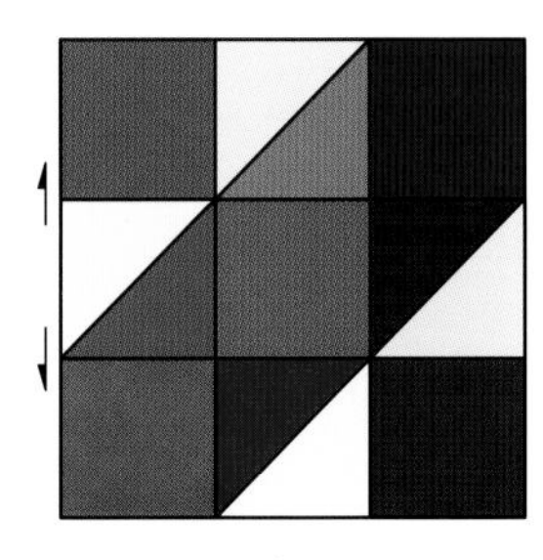

Make 12.

Assembling the Quilt Top

1. Refer to the quilt assembly diagram at right to arrange the blocks in five rows of five blocks each, alternating the blocks as shown. Sew the blocks into rows. Press the seam allowances toward the Contrary Wife blocks. Sew the rows together; press.
2. Sew remaining half-square-triangle units to opposite sides of a light square. Make eight units.

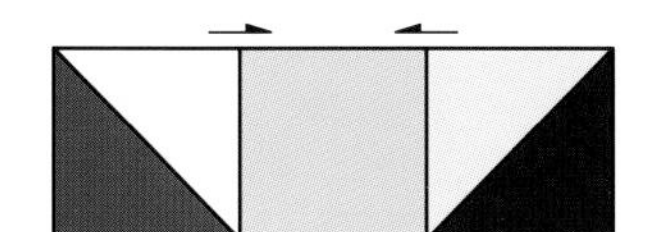

Make 8.

Pressing Tip

Do not press the seam allowances of the inner-border units until you sew them to the quilt. As you sew, direct the seam allowances so they oppose.

3. Arrange the units from step 2 and the remaining units from the Contrary Wife block into rows, alternating them as shown. Sew the units together. Make four rows. Referring to the quilt assembly diagram, sew rows to opposite sides of the quilt center. Sew a dark square to each end of the last two rows of partial blocks, and then sew these rows to the remaining sides of the quilt center.

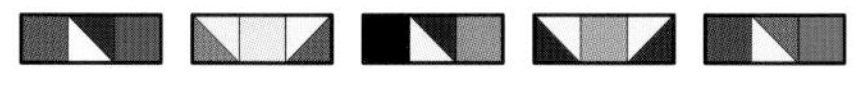

Side border.
Make 2.

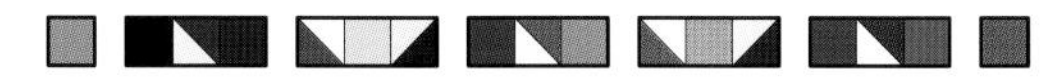

Top/bottom border.
Make 2.

4. Add the dark blue 4¾"-wide strips to the quilt top, referring to "Adding Borders" on page 15 to measure, cut, and sew them.

Quilt assembly

Finishing the Quilt

Refer to "Finishing Techniques" on page 16 for detailed instructions.

1. Layer the quilt top with the batting and backing; baste.
2. Hand or machine quilt. Follow the quilting suggestions shown below or use your own design.

Quilting diagram

3. Use the dark blue 2¼"-wide strips to bind the edges of your quilt.

Ahead of the **Game**

Pieced and quilted by Gayle Bong

For a handsome treatment of a single block, turn it into a medallion by adding several rounds of triangles and borders. This palette started with a charm pack of 5" squares, and then I added some matching scraps. The large floral was one of the prints in the pack. If you're stash busting, you could start by choosing the floral print, and then coordinating scraps to go with it.

Finished quilt: 48½" x 56½"

Finished block: 20"

Materials

Yardages are based on 42"-wide fabric.

1⅞ yards of multicolored print for setting triangles, outer border, and binding

⅞ yard *total* of assorted medium and dark scraps for center block and pieced border

⅝ yard of cream fabric 1 for setting triangles

½ yard of cream fabric 2 for center block and pieced border corner squares

½ yard *total* of assorted cream fabrics for pieced border

1 fat eighth (9" x 22") of cream fabric 3 for center block

1 square, 5¼" x 5¼", of cream fabric 4 for first round of block

3⅓ yards of fabric for backing

54" x 62" piece of batting

Cutting		
Please read all the instructions before starting. Cutting for the center block is separate from the setting triangles and borders so you can easily substitute a different center that finishes 20" square. For example, use four of the 10" Sparkling Star blocks made on page 64.		
FABRIC	FIRST CUT	FOLLOWING CUT
For the center block		
Cream 4	Cut the square into quarters diagonally to make 4 triangles	
Cream 3	4 squares, 2½" x 2½"	
	1 square, 5¼" x 5¼"	Cut the square into quarters diagonally to make 4 triangles
	4 squares, 2⅞" x 2⅞"	Cut each square in half diagonally to make 8 triangles
Cream 2	4 squares, 4½" x 4½"	
	4 squares, 4⅞" x 4⅞"	Cut each square in half diagonally to make 8 triangles
	16 squares, 2½" x 2½"	
Assorted medium and dark scraps	1 square, 4½" x 4½"	
	6 squares, 4⅞" x 4⅞"	Cut each square in half diagonally to make 12 triangles
	8 rectangles, 2½" x 4½"	
	8 squares, 2⅞" x 2⅞"	Cut each square in half diagonally to make 16 triangles
For the setting triangles and borders		
Multicolored print	1 square, 21¼" x 21¼"	Cut the square into quarters diagonally to make 4 setting triangles
	5 strips, 4½" x 42"	
	6 strips, 2¼" x 42"	
Cream 1	2 squares, 16⅞" x 16⅞"	Cut each square in half diagonally to make 4 triangles
Assorted creams	18 squares, 4⅞" x 4⅞"	Cut each square in half diagonally to make 36 triangles
Cream 2	4 squares, 4½" x 4½"	
Assorted medium and dark scraps	16 squares, 4⅞" x 4⅞"	Cut each square in half diagonally to make 32 triangles

Making the Center Block

After sewing each seam, press the seam allowances in the direction indicated by the arrows.

1. Sew cream 4 triangles to opposite sides of the 4½" medium or dark square; press. Repeat with the remaining two sides.

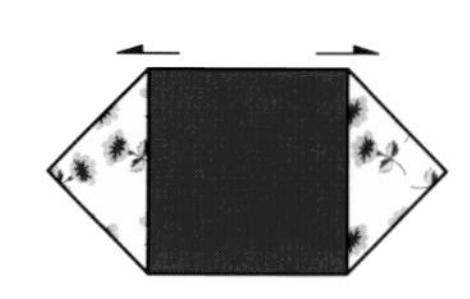
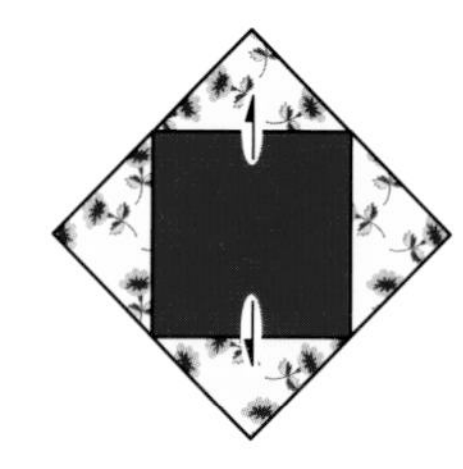

Make 1.

2. Sew 4⅞" medium or dark triangles to opposite sides of the square made in step 1; press. Repeat with the remaining two sides.

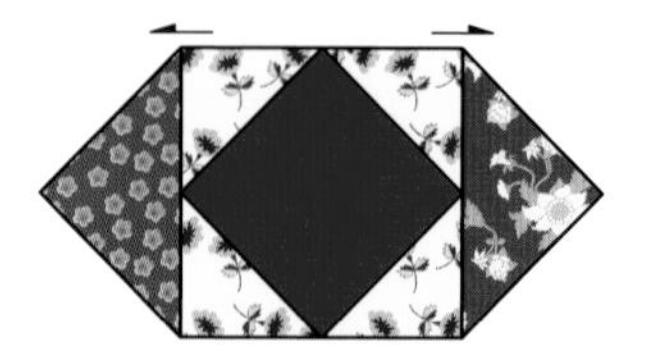
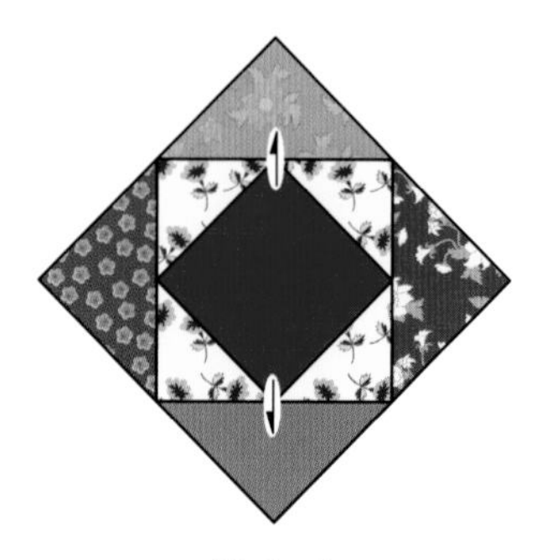

Make 1.

3. Using the 2⅞" triangles, sew a cream 3 triangle to a medium or dark triangle to make a half-square-triangle unit. Make eight units.

Make 8.

4. Sew 2⅞" medium or dark triangles to both short edges of a 5¼" cream 3 triangle to make a flying-geese unit. Make four units.

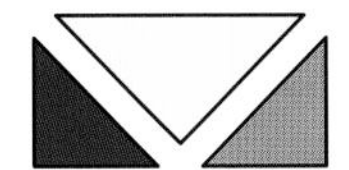
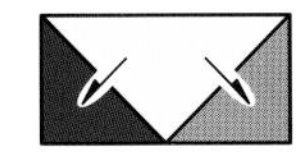

Make 4.

5. Sew a half-square-triangle unit from step 3 to each end of each flying-geese unit as shown. Add 2½" cream 3 squares to the ends of two of the strips. Add these units to the unit from step 2. Press the seam allowances open.

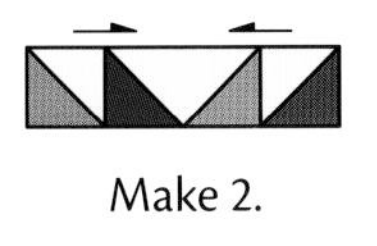

Make 2.

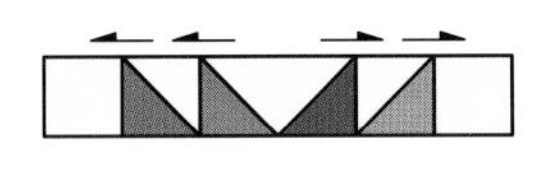

Make 2.

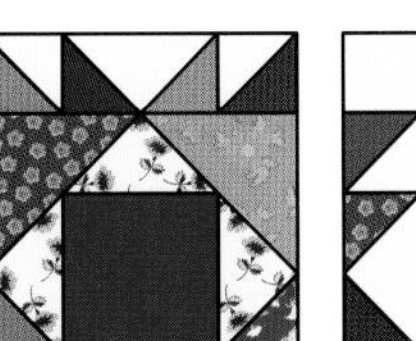

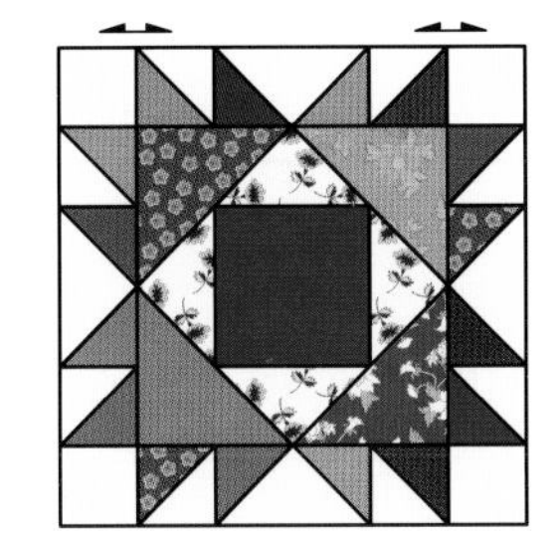

Make 1.

6. Draw a diagonal line from corner to corner on the wrong side of the 2½" cream 2 squares. With right sides together and edges matched, place a cream square on one end of a 2½" x 4½" medium or dark rectangle. Stitch on the drawn line. Trim the seam allowances to ¼"; press. Repeat with another cream square on the opposite end of the rectangle. Make eight flying-geese units. Sew two units together to make a double flying-geese unit. Make four double units.

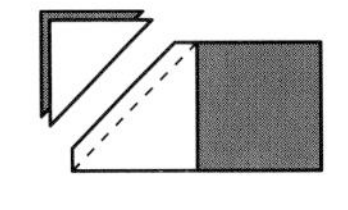
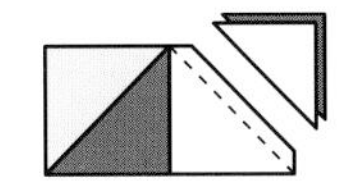
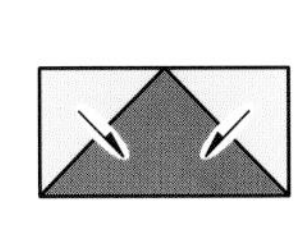

Make 8.

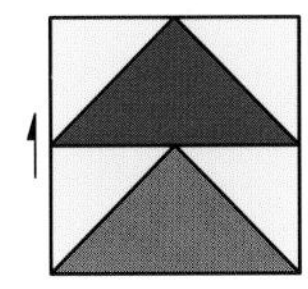

Make 4.

7. Using the 4⅞" triangles, sew a cream 2 triangle to a medium or dark triangle. Make eight half-square-triangle units.

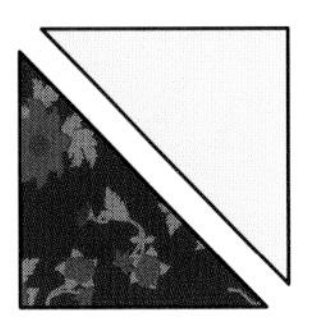

Make 8.

8. Sew half-square-triangle units to the ends of each double flying-geese unit. Add 4½" cream 2 squares to the ends of two of the units. Add these units to the center block. Press these seam allowances open.

Make 1.

Assembling the Quilt Top

1. Fold each multicolored print triangle in half along the long edge and finger-press a crease. With the creases matched to the center points at the edges of the block, sew triangles to opposite sides of the block. Repeat for the remaining two sides.

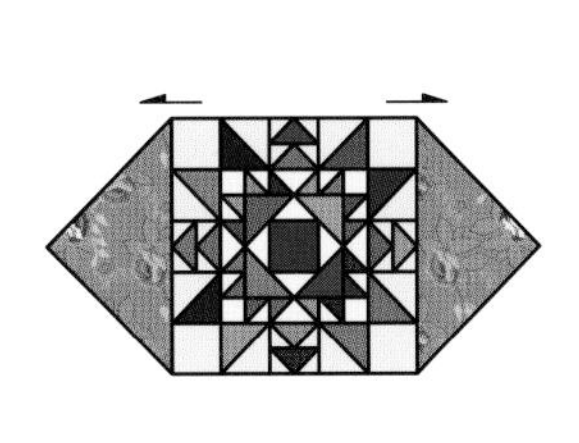

2. Sew a 4⅞" assorted cream triangle to a 4⅞" medium or dark triangle to make a half-square-triangle unit. Make 32 half-square-triangle units.

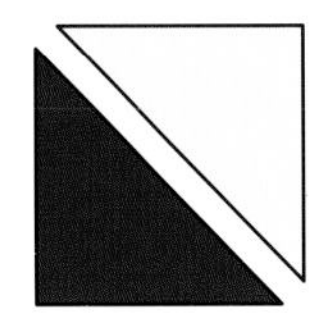
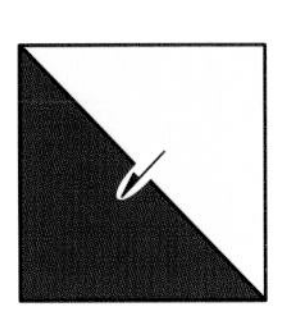

Make 32.

3. Join four half-square-triangle units side by side as shown to make a border unit. Make four. Repeat to make four border units with four triangle units facing in the opposite direction.

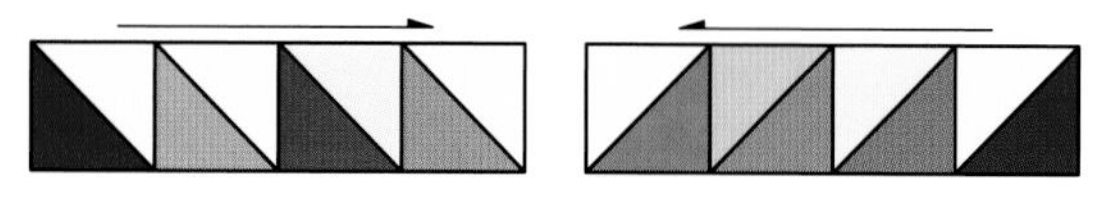

Make 4 of each.

4. Sew 4⅞" assorted cream triangles to the border units from step 3. Sew each border unit to a 16⅞" cream 1 triangle as shown.

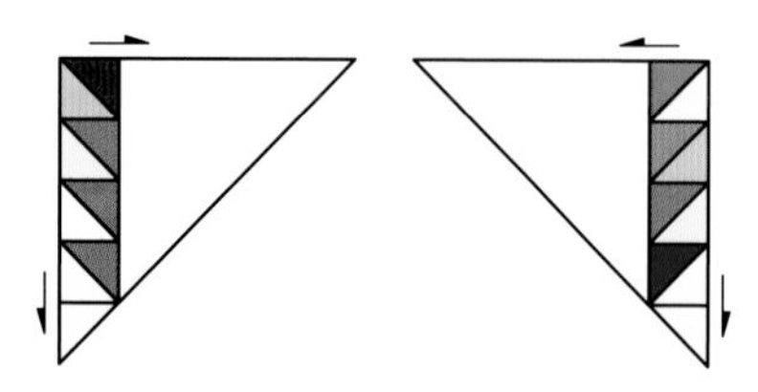

Make 2 of each.

5. Sew the units from step 4 to opposite sides of the quilt top, matching centers as before. Repeat for the remaining two sides.

6. Sew one of each of the remaining units from step 3 together with two 4½" cream 2 squares as shown. Make two border strips. Sew the strips to the top and bottom edges of the quilt top.

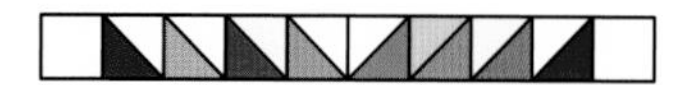

Top/bottom border.
Make 2.

7. Attach the 4½"-wide multicolored print strips to the quilt top, referring to "Adding Borders" on page 15 to measure, cut, and sew them.

Quilt assembly

Finishing the Quilt

Refer to "Finishing Techniques" on page 16 for detailed instructions.

1. Layer the quilt top with the batting and backing; baste.
2. Hand or machine quilt. Follow the quilting suggestions shown below or use your own design.

Quilting diagram

3. Use the 2¼"-wide multicolored print strips to bind the edges of your quilt.

Cutting-Room **Floor**

Pieced and quilted by Gayle Bong

When I started this quilt, every small triangle was already cut and waiting patiently for me to find the time and the perfect design in which to use it. Light and dark triangles that finish to 2" can be cut from your collection of 2½"-wide strips using a triangle-cutting ruler. Don't forget to scrounge around in your scrap box for small pieces to cut into triangles first.

Finished quilt: 60½" x 60½"

Finished block: 8"

Materials

Yardages are based on 42"-wide fabric.

1¾ yards of medium-light pink fabric for blocks

1¾ yards of dark blue fabric for border and binding

1½ yards *total* of assorted dark scraps for blocks

1 yard *total* of assorted light scraps for blocks

3¾ yards of fabric for backing

66" x 66" piece of batting

Cutting

Please read all the instructions before starting.

FABRIC	FIRST CUT	FOLLOWING CUT(S)
Assorted light scraps	17 strips, ⅞" x 20"*	102 squares, 2⅞" x 2⅞"; cut each square in half diagonally to make 204 triangles
Assorted dark scraps	30 strips, 2⅞" x 20"*	178 squares, 2⅞" x 2⅞"; cut each square in half diagonally to make 356 triangles
Medium-light pink	3 strips, 8⅞" x 42"	10 squares, 8⅞" x 8⅞"; cut each square in half diagonally to make 20 triangles
	4 strips, 4½" x 42"	4 rectangles, 4½" x 16⅞"
		4 rectangles, 4½" x 12⅞"
		4 squares, 4½" x 4½"
	1 square, 9¼" x 9¼"	Cut the square into quarters diagonally to make 4 triangles
	2 squares, 4⅞" x 4⅞"	Cut each square in half diagonally to make 4 triangles
Dark blue	6 strips, 6½" x 42"	
	7 strips, 2¼" x 42"	

**Refer to "Cutting Triangles Using a Triangle-Cutting Ruler" on page 13 for an alternate way to cut the triangles from 2½" strips.*

Working with Bias

The bias edge of a triangle tends to stretch, and the larger the triangle the more likely that it will stretch. It's helpful to use spray starch to stabilize the pink fabric *before* cutting to minimize the stretching.

Making the Little Lady Blocks

After sewing each seam, press the seam allowances in the direction indicated by the arrows.

1. Sew a light 2⅞" triangle to a dark 2⅞" triangle to make a half-square-triangle unit. Make 204 units.

Make 204.

2. Sew dark 2⅞" triangles to adjacent light edges of a half-square-triangle unit. Repeat to make a total of 44 triangle units.

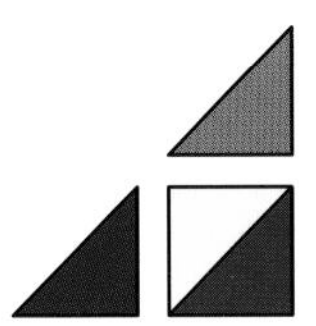
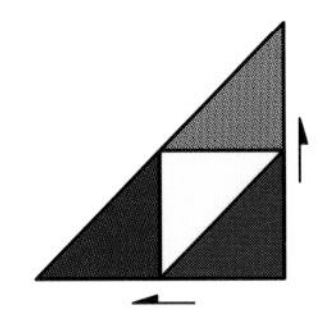

Make 44.

3. Arrange one triangle unit from step 2, five half-square-triangle units from step 1, and two dark triangles into three rows as shown. Sew the pieces in the second and third rows together, and then sew these two rows together. Add the triangle unit to the top of the joined rows. Make 32 Little Lady half-block units. Set aside the 12 remaining triangle units for the Sparkling Star block.

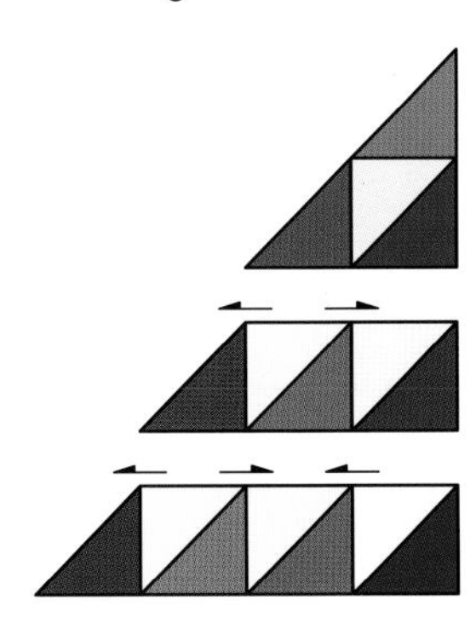
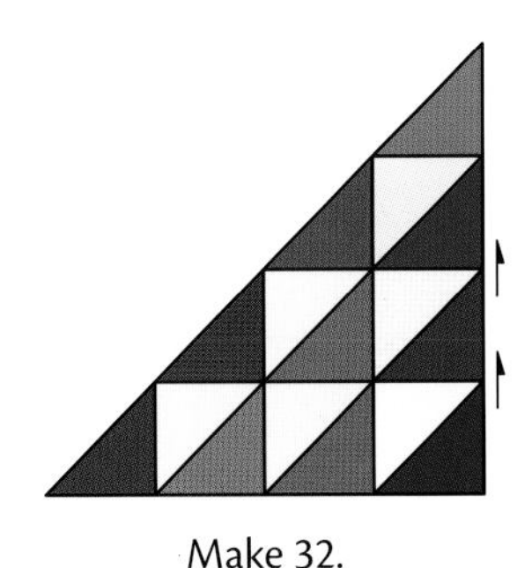

Make 32.

4. Sew a Little Lady half-block unit from step 3 to a pink 8⅞" triangle to make a Little Lady block. Make 20 blocks. Set aside the remaining Little Lady half-block units.

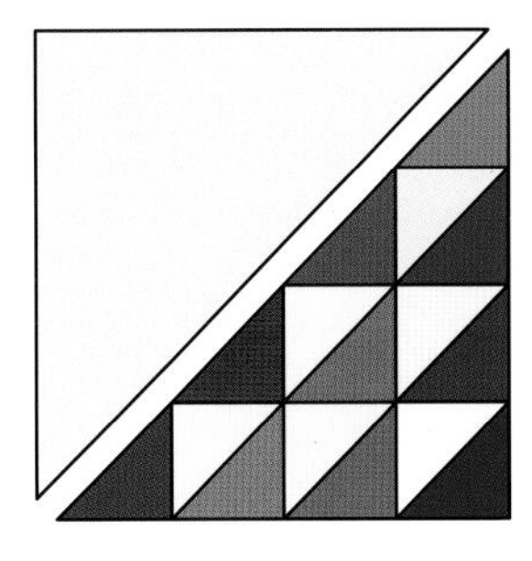
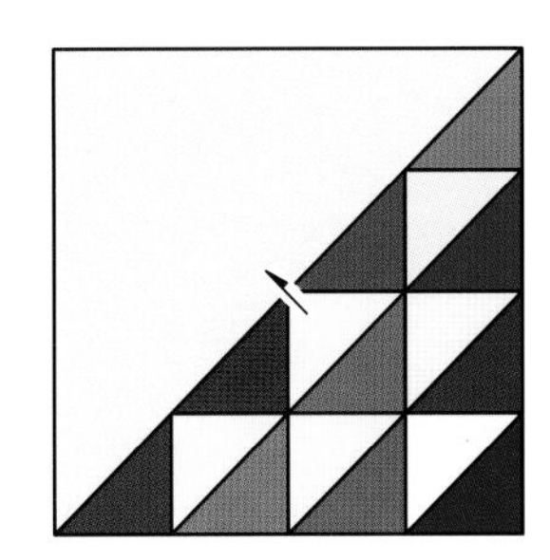

Little Lady block.
Make 20.

Making the Sparkling Star Block

1. Sew a triangle unit from step 2 of "Making the Little Lady Blocks" to a pink 4⅞" triangle. Make four units. Join the units as shown to make the block center.

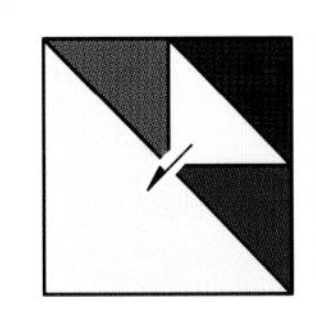

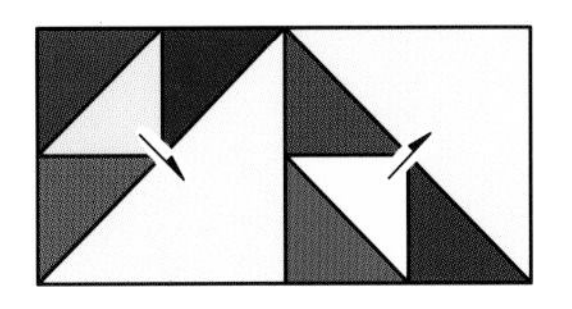
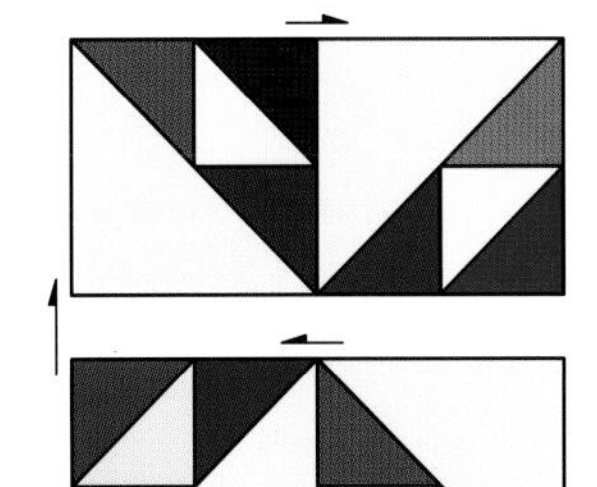

Make 1.

2. Sew a triangle unit to opposite sides of a pink 9¼" triangle to make a star-point unit. Make four units.

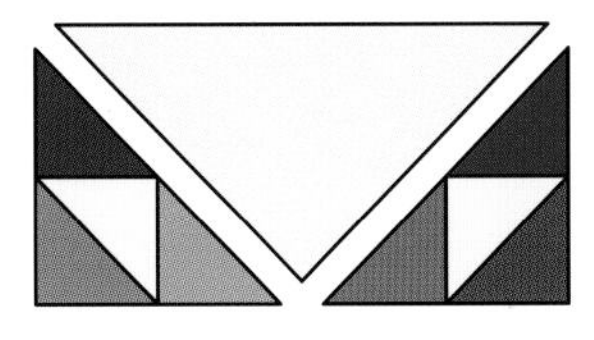
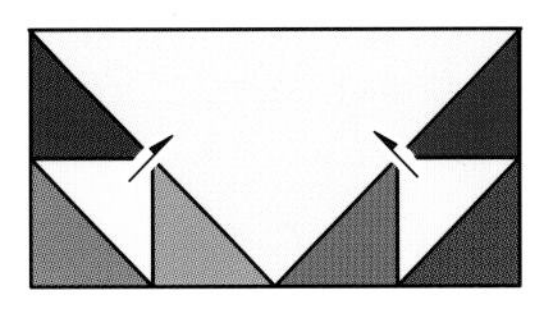

Make 4.

3. Lay out four pink 4½" squares, the star-points units, and the block center. Sew the units into rows, and then sew the rows together to make the Sparkling Star block.

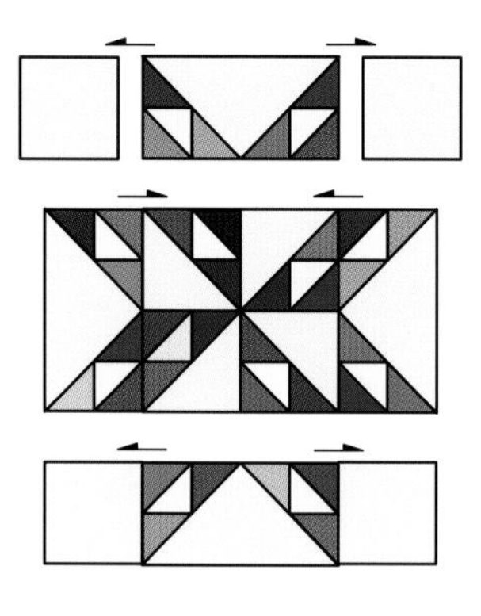
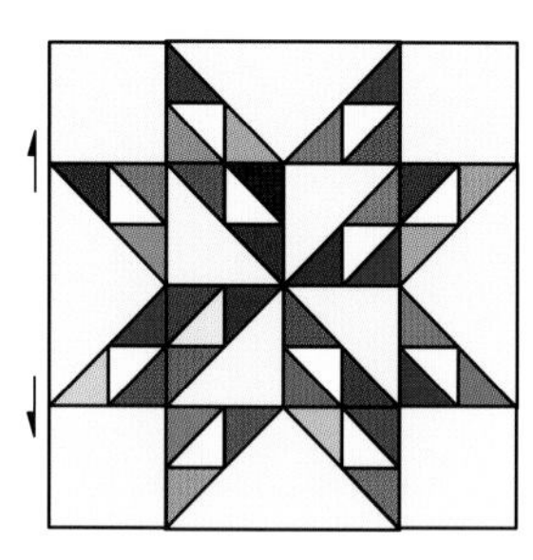

Sparkling Star block.
Make 1.

Assembling the Quilt Top

1. Sew together two of the remaining Little Lady half-block units to make a large pieced triangle unit. Make four units.

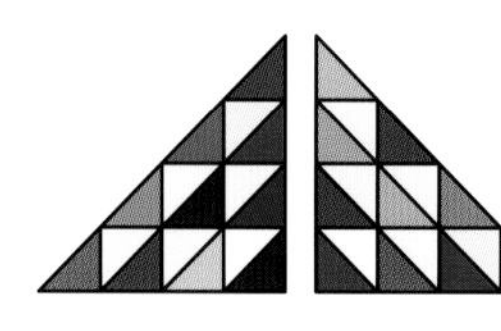
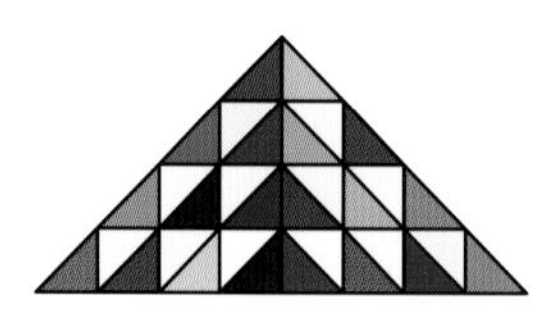

Make 4.

2. Sew two large pieced triangle units to opposite sides of the Sparkling Star block. Repeat for the remaining two sides.

3. With right sides up, trim a 45° triangle from the end of each pink 4½" x 12⅞" rectangle and each pink 4½" x 16⅞" rectangle as shown to make trapezoids.

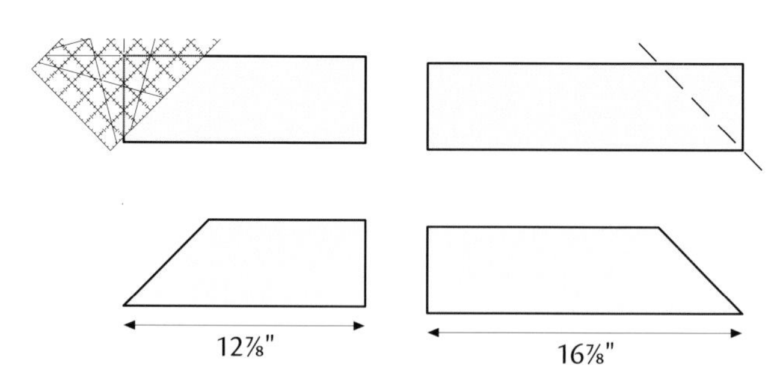

4. Sew a 12⅞"-wide trapezoid to the bottom of a Little Lady half-block unit. Add a 16⅞"-wide trapezoid to the right edge. Make four corner units.

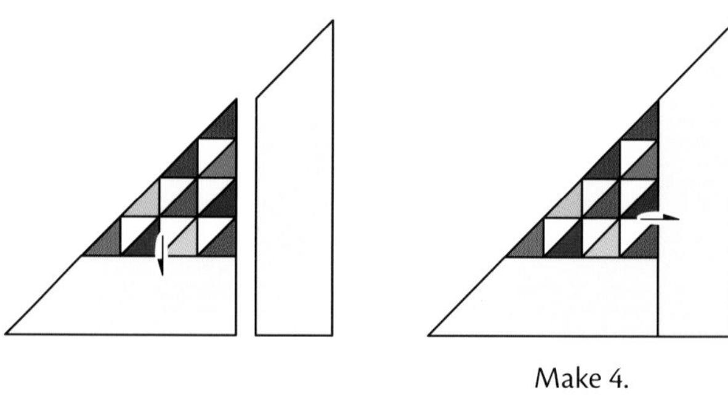

Make 4.

5. Sew corner units to opposite sides of the unit from step 2. Repeat on the remaining two sides.

6. Sew four Little Lady blocks together to make a side border. Make two borders. Add these to the sides of the quilt center. Sew six Little Lady blocks together to make the top border. Repeat to make the bottom border. Add these to the top and bottom edges of the quilt center.

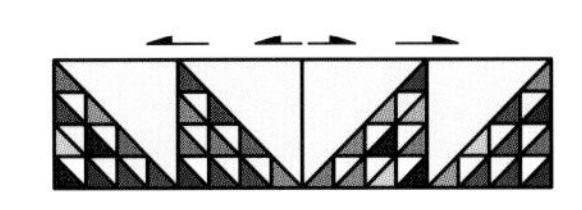

Side border.
Make 2.

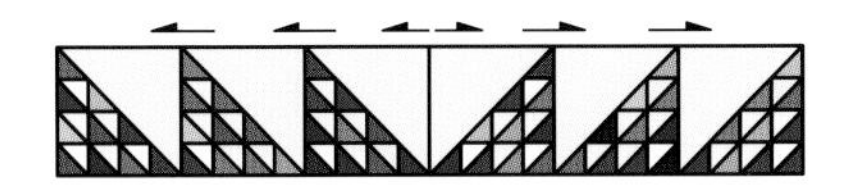

Top/bottom border.
Make 2.

7. Add the dark blue 6½"-wide strips to the quilt top, referring to "Adding Borders" on page 15 to measure, cut, and sew them.

Quilt assembly

Finishing the Quilt

Refer to "Finishing Techniques" on page 16 for detailed instructions.

1. Layer the quilt top with the batting and backing; baste.
2. Hand or machine quilt. Follow the quilting suggestions shown below or use your own design.

Quilting diagram

3. Use the dark blue 2¼"-wide strips to bind the edges of your quilt.

Sparkling **Stars** in Taupe

Pieced and quilted by Gayle Bong

The color taupe has a sophisticated look that's a perfect companion to the classic Sparkling Stars block. A 5" charm pack of taupe fabrics was the impetus for this design. I needed to add a few more colors to get the range of values I wanted. It's the dark that makes the light sparkle. You could choose any style of fabric, so consider the character or mood you want for your quilt first.

Finished quilt: 62" x 62"

Finished block: 10"

Materials

Yardages are based on 42"-wide fabric.

2 yards *total* of assorted dark taupe scraps for blocks

1¾ yards of light taupe fabric for block backgrounds

1 yard of dark taupe fabric for outer border

½ yard *total* of assorted cream scraps for Sparkling Star blocks

⅜ yard of cream fabric for Sparkling Star block centers

⅜ yard of teal fabric for inner border

½ yard of fabric for binding

4 yards of fabric for backing

68" x 68" piece of batting

6" Bias Square® ruler

Cutting

Please read all the instructions before starting.

FABRIC	FIRST CUT	FOLLOWING CUT(S)
Assorted cream scraps	20 squares, 5" x 5"	
Assorted dark taupe scraps	20 squares, 5" x 5"	
	6 squares, 11¼" x 11¼"	Cut each square into quarters diagonally to make 24 large triangles
	39 squares, 5" x 5"	156 squares, 2⅛" x 2⅛"; cut each square in half diagonally to make 312 small triangles
Cream (block centers)	3 strips, 3⅜" x 42"	26 squares, 3⅜" x 3⅜"; cut each square in half diagonally to make 52 triangles
Light taupe	4 strips, 3" x 42"	52 squares, 3" x 3"
	3 strips, 6¼" x 42"	13 squares, 6¼" x 6¼"; cut each square into quarters diagonally to make 52 triangles
	6 squares, 11¼" x 11¼"	Cut each square into quarters diagonally to make 24 triangles
Teal	6 strips, 1¾" x 42"	
Dark taupe	6 strips, 5" x 42"	
Binding fabric	7 strips, 2¼" x 42"	

Making the Sparkling Star Blocks

After sewing each seam, press the seam allowances in the direction indicated by the arrows.

1. Place a cream scrap 5" square and a dark taupe scrap 5" square right sides together with raw edges even. Cut the squares in half diagonally. Cut the resulting triangles 1¾" from and parallel to the diagonal cut. This will create two pairs of short bias strips ready to sew and four triangles from each pair of squares. Cut all 40 squares. Sew the pairs of cream and taupe short bias strips together ¼" away from their longest bias edge, and then add a different print triangle to the short bias edges. Press the seam allowances open to minimize bulk. Make 40 bias-strip units.

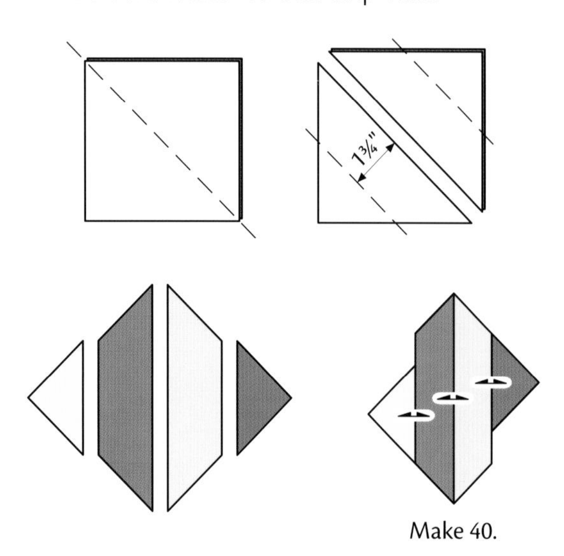

Make 40.

2. You'll be cutting four half-square-triangle units from each bias-strip unit. The finished cut size of each square will be 1¾", but because the edges of the bias square aren't all even, you may need to cut the squares slightly larger than that, and then trim them to size. Begin by positioning a bias-square unit on your cutting mat as shown above right. Starting at the lower-left corner, align the 45° line of the Bias Square ruler with the center seam line. Cut along the side and top edge of the ruler to separate the half-square-triangle unit from the rest of the fabric. Rotate the half-square-triangle unit and cut the remaining two sides to square it up to 1¾" if necessary. Continue to cut three more half-square-triangle units from the bias-square unit. Repeat with the remaining bias-strip units to cut a total of 160 half-square-triangle units.

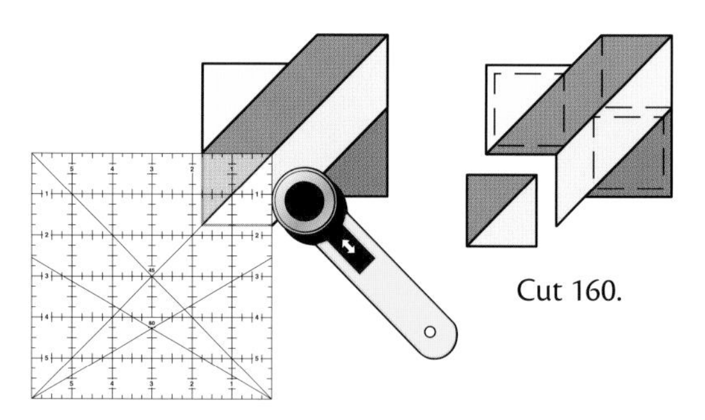
Cut 160.

3. Sew small dark taupe triangles to adjacent light edges of a half-square-triangle unit. Make 156 triangle units. Set aside the remaining half-square-triangle units for another project.

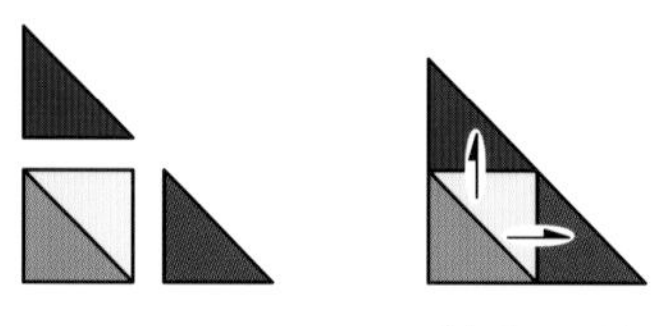
Make 156.

4. Sew a triangle unit to each cream 3⅜" triangle. Stitch four of these units together to make a block-center unit. Make 13 units.

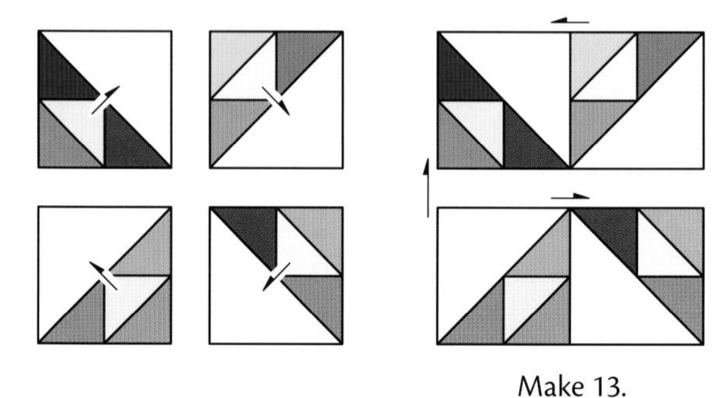
Make 13.

5. Sew triangle units to both short edges of a cream 6¼" triangle to make a star-point unit. Make 52 units.

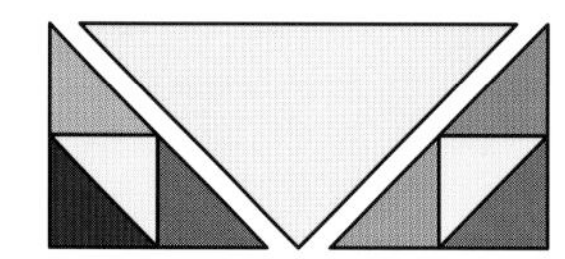
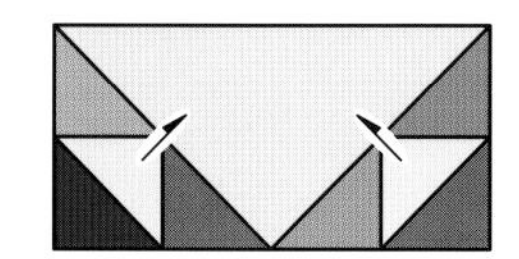
Make 52.

6. Sew four star-point units, a center unit, and four light taupe 3" squares into rows. Sew the rows together to make a Sparkling Star block. Make 13 blocks.

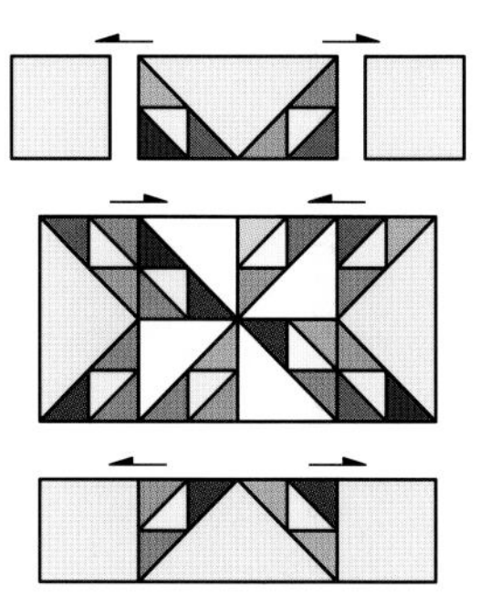

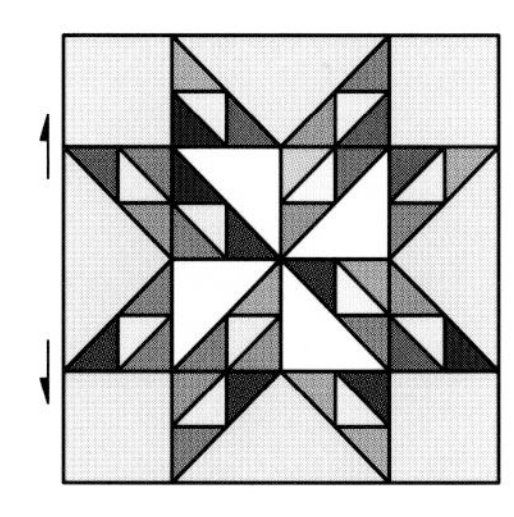

Make 13.

Making the Hourglass Blocks

Sew two light taupe and two dark taupe triangles together as shown to make a block; press. Make 12 Hourglass blocks.

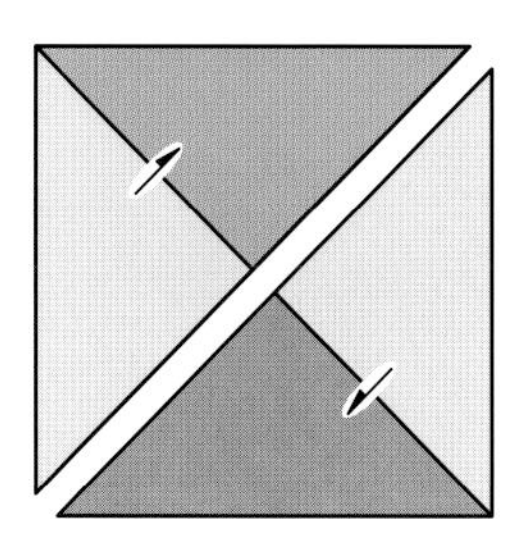

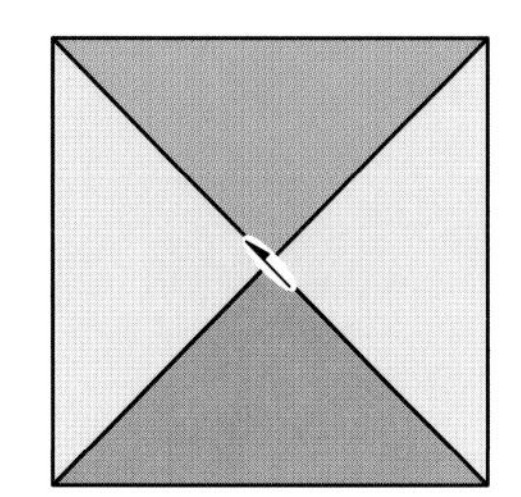

Make 12.

Assembling the Quilt Top

1. Arrange the blocks in five rows of five blocks each, alternating the blocks in each row and from row to row. Rotate the Hourglass blocks as shown. Sew the blocks into rows, and then sew the rows together.
2. Attach the teal 1¾"-wide inner-border strips to the quilt top, referring to "Adding Borders" on page 15 to measure, cut, and sew them. Repeat with the dark taupe 5"-wide outer-border strips.

Quilt assembly

Finishing the Quilt

Refer to "Finishing Techniques" on page 16 for detailed instructions.

1. Layer the quilt top with the batting and backing; baste.
2. Hand or machine quilt. Follow the quilting suggestions shown below or use your own design.

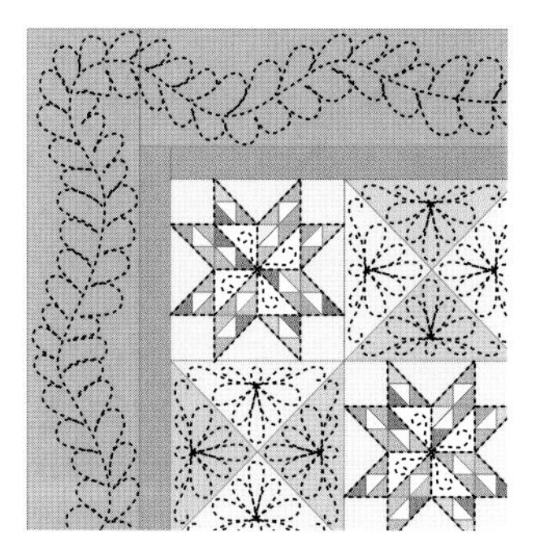

Quilting diagram

3. Use the 2¼"-wide strips to bind the edges of your quilt.

Friday-Night **Special**

Pieced and quilted by Gayle Bong

The Chimney Sweep block has been a favorite of mine for years; I can't believe it has taken me this long to use it in a quilt. I worked on this on Friday evenings when my friends were over. No wonder I think it's so special. Choose your favorite fabrics and make your quilt special too. Choose 30 dark strips, 2" x 42" or 4" x 21". If you're short on scraps, consider substituting 2½ yards of just one purchased fabric for the scrappy alternate dark squares and setting triangles.

Finished quilt: 69½" x 81½"

Finished block: 8½"

Materials

Yardages are based on 42"-wide fabric.

4⅜ yards *total* of assorted dark scraps for blocks, setting squares, and setting triangles

2⅛ yards of muslin for blocks and inner border

1½ yards of blue fabric for outer border and binding

5½ yards of fabric for backing

78" x 90" piece of batting

Cutting		
Please read all the instructions before starting.		
FABRIC	FIRST CUT	FOLLOWING CUT(S)
Assorted dark scraps	20 squares, 9" x 9"	
	18 side setting triangles*	
	2 squares, 8" x 8"	Cut *each* square in half diagonally to make 4 corner setting triangles
	30 strips, 2" x 34"	Cut *each* strip into 4 rectangles (120 total), 2" x 5", and 8 squares (240 total), 2" x 2"
Muslin	3 strips, 2" x 42"	60 squares, 2" x 2"
	4 strips, 2" x 42"	30 rectangles, 2" x 5"
	9 strips, 3⅜" x 42"	90 squares, 3⅜" x 3⅜"; cut each square into quarters diagonally to make 360 large triangles
	3 strips, 2" x 42"	60 squares, 2" x 2"; cut each square in half diagonally to make 120 small triangles
	8 strips, 2" x 42"	
Blue	8 strips, 3½" x 42"	
	8 strips, 2¼" x 42"	
**From freezer paper or newspaper, cut a 13¼" square into quarters diagonally to make four triangles. Use one paper triangle as a template to cut the side setting triangles.*		

Smart Move to Avoid Problems

Consider making a sample block to check your seam allowance before cutting the setting squares and triangles. Or, if you have enough scraps, cut the setting squares and triangles after you've made and measured the pieced blocks to find the average size to cut the pieces.

Making the Chimney Sweep Blocks

Keep matching fabrics together so one print is used in each block. After sewing each seam, press the seam allowances in the direction indicated by the arrows.

1. Arrange four matching dark squares, two muslin squares, and one muslin rectangle as shown. Sew the squares into rows, and then sew the rows together.

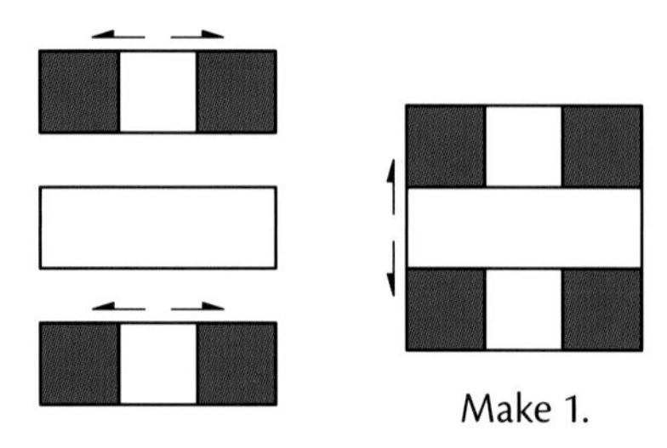

Make 1.

2. Sew a dark square between two large muslin triangles. Sew this unit between a dark rectangle and a small muslin triangle. Make four units. Sew large muslin triangles to opposite ends of the dark rectangle on two of the units.

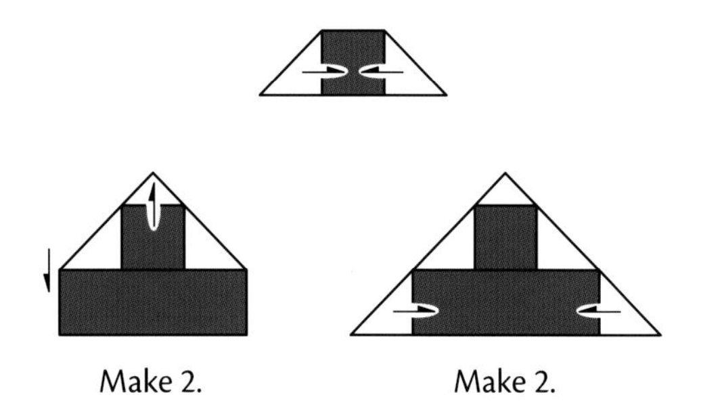

Make 2. Make 2.

3. Arrange the units from steps 1 and 2 in diagonal rows. Sew the center row together, and then add the corner units to complete the block. Square up the block to 9" x 9".

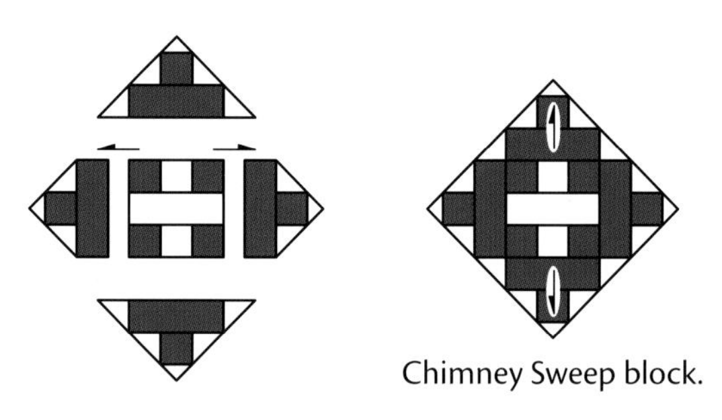

Chimney Sweep block.

4. Repeat steps 1–3 to make a total of 30 blocks.

Assembling the Quilt Top

1. Arrange the Chimney Sweep blocks, the dark 9" setting squares, the dark side setting triangles, and the dark corner setting triangles into diagonal rows. Sew the pieces in each row together. Press the seam allowances toward the setting squares. Sew the rows together. Add the corner setting triangles last; press.

2. Square up the corners of the quilt top, trimming the edges 1/4" past the corners of the blocks.
3. Attach the muslin 2"-wide inner-border strips to the quilt top, referring to "Adding Borders" on page 15 to measure, cut, and sew them. Repeat with the blue 3½"-wide outer-border strips.

Quilt assembly

Finishing the Quilt

Refer to "Finishing Techniques" on page 16 for detailed instructions.

1. Layer the quilt top with the batting and backing; baste.
2. Hand or machine quilt. Follow the quilting suggestions shown below or use your own design.

Quilting diagram

3. Use the blue 2¼"-wide strips to bind the edges of your quilt.

County Fair

Pieced and quilted by Gayle Bong

It was a challenge for me to use the large-scale multicolored print in this quilt, but I enjoyed it. Isolating it from the background fabric was necessary to avoid losing the pattern. Choose the multicolored print first and look carefully at the range of colors in it. Mine read primarily purple, so I was surprised to see all the blue in it. My coordinating darks were cut from 2½"-wide strips using a triangle-cutting ruler (see page 13).

Finished quilt: 44½" x 44½"

Finished block: 12"

Materials

Yardages are based on 42"-wide fabric.

1⅜ yards *total* of assorted dark purple scraps for blocks

1 yard of light fabric for block and border backgrounds

⅝ yard of large-scale multicolored print for blocks

⅛ yard *total* of assorted accent scraps for block centers

½ yard of fabric for binding

3 yards of fabric for backing

50" x 50" piece of batting

Cutting		
Please read all the instructions before starting.		
FABRIC	FIRST CUT	FOLLOWING CUT(S)
Assorted accent scraps	9 squares, 3⅜" x 3⅜"	
Multicolored print	5 strips, 3⅜" x 42"	36 rectangles, 3⅜" x 5"
Light	4 strips, 4⅞" x 42"	32 squares, 4⅞" x 4⅞"; cut each square in half diagonally to make 64 triangles
	4 strips, 2½" x 42"	36 rectangles, 2½" x 4½"
Assorted dark purple scraps	9 strips, 2⅞" x 29"*	4 squares, 2⅞" x 2⅞", from each strip; cut each square in half diagonally to make 8 small triangles (72 total). From the remainder of each strip, cut 4 large quarter-square triangles (36 total).**
	24 rectangles, 2½" x 13¼"	
	2 squares, 4⅞" x 4⅞"	Cut each square once diagonally to make 4 triangles.
Binding	5 strips, 2¼" x 42"	

Refer to "Cutting Triangles Using a Triangle-Cutting Ruler" on page 13 for an alternate way to cut the half-square triangles from 2½"-wide strips.

***Refer to "Cutting Triangles Using a Triangle-Cutting Ruler" on page 13 for an alternate way to cut the quarter-square triangles from 2½"-wide strips or follow these instructions to cut the 2⅞"-wide strips: Place the 45° line of your ruler on the long edge of the strip and make the first cut near the lower-left corner of the strip. Take the piece you've just cut and put it in your scrap stash. Rotate the ruler so it's perpendicular to the first cut, place the 45° line on the bottom edge of the strip, and align the cutting edge of the ruler with the top edge of the strip to form a triangle; cut. Repeat the process, alternating the ruler between these positions to cut the four triangles needed from each strip.*

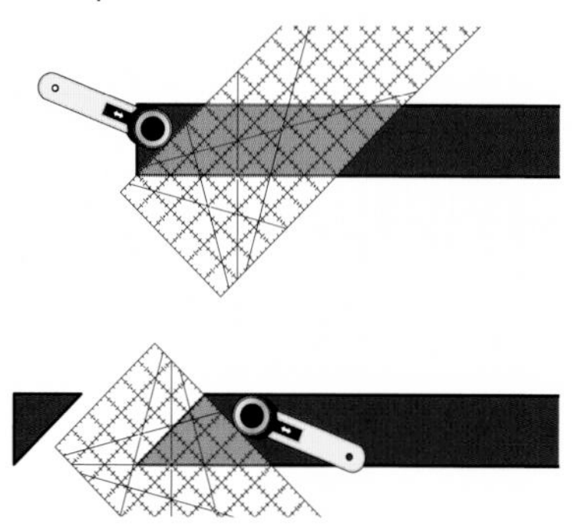

Making the Blocks

Keep matching fabrics together so one dark fabric is used in each block. After sewing each seam, press the seam allowances in the direction indicated.

1. Sew one accent square, four large-scale multicolored print rectangles, and four identical large dark purple triangles together.

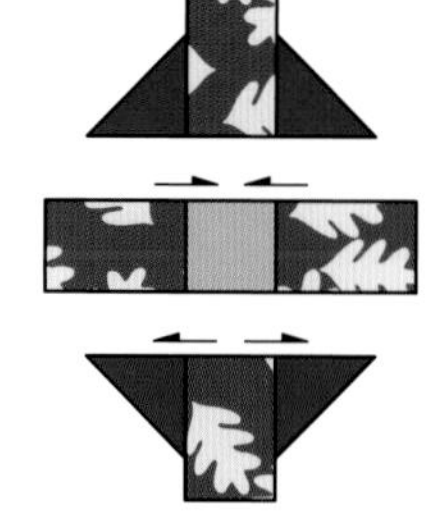

2. Square the units to 8½" x 8½", measuring 4¼" from the center point to trim each edge. If possible, use a large square ruler so you can measure and cut two edges without moving the ruler.

3. Sew a matching small dark triangle to each end of a light rectangle. Make four units.

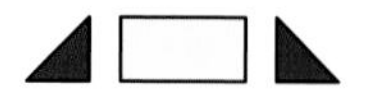

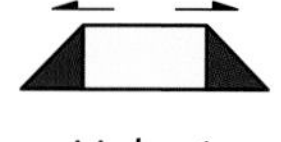

Make 4.

4. Sew the units from step 3 to each side of the unit from step 2. Sew a light triangle to each corner.

5. Repeat steps 1–4 to make a total of nine blocks.

Assembling the Quilt Top

1. Sew the dark purple rectangles together in pairs. Trim a 45° triangle from each end of the rectangle pairs to make trapezoids.

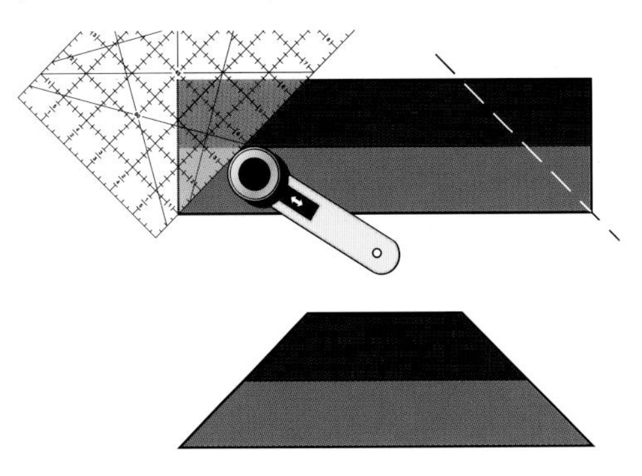

Make 12.

2. Sew a light triangle to each angled edge of the trapezoid units.

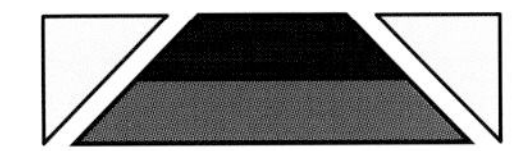

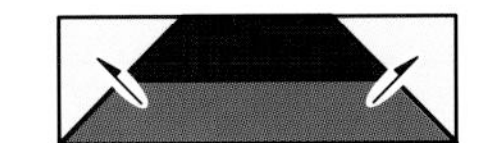

3. Sew one each of the remaining dark and light triangles together to make a half-square-triangle unit. Make four units for the quilt corners.

Make 4.

4. Arrange the County Fair blocks into three rows of three blocks each. Place the border and corner units around the blocks as shown. Sew the blocks and border units into rows, and then sew the rows together.

Quilt assembly

5. Stay stitch 1/8" from the quilt edges. This will prevent the seams in the pieced border from coming apart around the edge of the quilt.

Finishing the Quilt

Refer to "Finishing Techniques" on page 16 for detailed instructions.

1. Layer the quilt top with the batting and backing; baste.
2. Hand or machine quilt. Follow the quilting suggestions shown below or use your own design.

Quilting diagram

3. Use the 2¼"-wide strips to bind the edges of your quilt.

Fast **Friends**

Pieced and quilted by Gayle Bong

Finished quilt: 42½" x 42½"

Finished block: 6"

I made the Thirtysomething Star blocks, and then stashed them in a box in the closet. Apparently I did the same with the Square-in-a-Square blocks. A few years later I cleaned the closet and found I had two piles of blocks the same size! Then I planned an easy border unit to complete the design nicely. You'll need dark, medium, or bright 2½"-wide strips and 3" finished triangles.

Materials

Yardages are based on 42"-wide fabric.

1⅞ yards *total* of assorted medium and dark scraps for blocks and border

1½ yards *total* of assorted cream scraps for blocks and border

½ yard of fabric for binding

2⅞ yards of fabric for backing

48" x 48" piece of batting

Thirtysomething Square Up tool (optional; available at www.gaylebong.com)

Cutting

Please read all the instructions before starting.

FABRIC	FIRST CUT	FOLLOWING CUT(S)
Assorted cream scraps	5 strips, 3½" x 42"	26 rectangles, 3½" x 6"; cut each rectangle in half diagonally to make 52 C triangles
	12 squares, 4¾" x 4¾"	
	3 strips, 3¾" x 42"	
	2 rectangles, 5½" x 9½"	Cut each rectangle in half diagonally to make 4 corner triangles
Assorted medium and dark scraps	18 strips, 2½" x 20"	72 rectangles, 2½" x 4¼"
	24 squares, 3⅞" x 3⅞"*	Cut each square once diagonally to make 48 triangles
	40 rectangles, 3½" x 5"	
	8 different rectangles, 4¼" x 7¼"	With pairs of rectangles *wrong sides together*, cut in half diagonally to make 16 triangles. Use 1 of each print.
Binding fabric	5 strips, 2¼" x 42"	

**Refer to "Cutting Triangles Using a Triangle-Cutting Ruler" on page 13 for an alternate way to cut triangles from 3½" strips.*

Making the Thirtysomething Star Blocks

After sewing each seam, press the seam allowances in the direction indicated by the arrows.

1. With right sides up, divide the medium and dark 2½" x 4¼" rectangles into two stacks with 36 rectangles in each. Cut the rectangle in one stack in half diagonally from lower left to upper right to make 72 A triangles. Cut the rectangles in the remaining stack in half diagonally from upper left to lower right to make 72 B triangles. Label each stack of triangles.

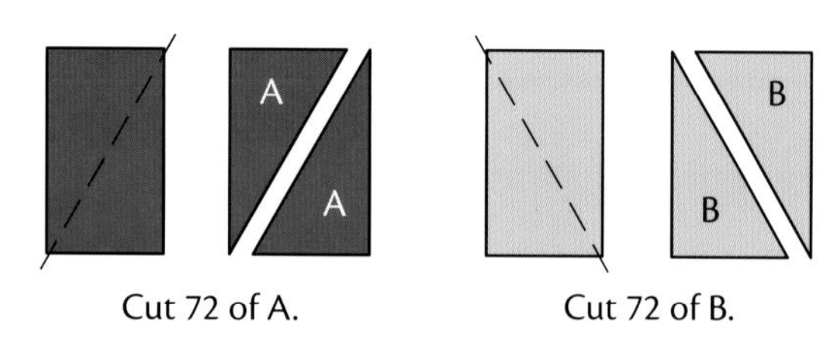

Cut 72 of A. Cut 72 of B.

2. Match the points of a dark A triangle with a cream C triangle. Start stitching the triangles together at the broad end of the cream C triangles. The smaller A triangle will be underneath. Hold the point straight while pressing the seam allowances toward the A triangle. Press carefully to avoid tucks, particularly at the point. Do not trim the point until after the next step. Make 52 units.

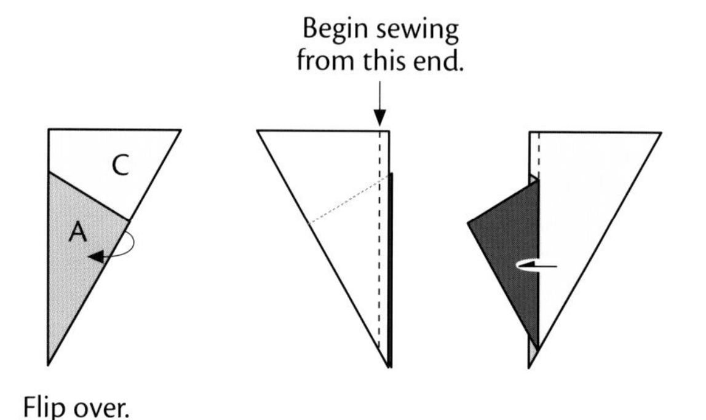

Flip over.

Points to Remember

Be sure to sew on the long bias edge of the A and B triangles. The broad end of the C triangle will point in one direction, and then the other. Ignore this as you sew; the excess fabric will be trimmed off later.

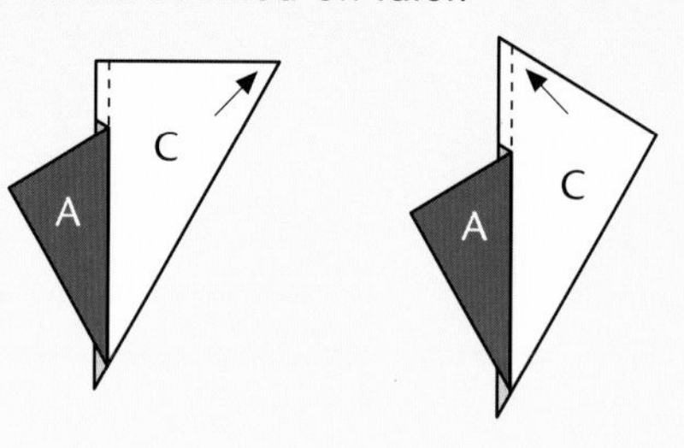

3. Place a dark B triangle right sides together with the cream triangle of a unit from step 1, aligning the raw edges of the three narrow points. Start stitching at the broad end of the cream triangle. Press the seam allowances toward the B triangle. Make 52 small Thirtysomething units.

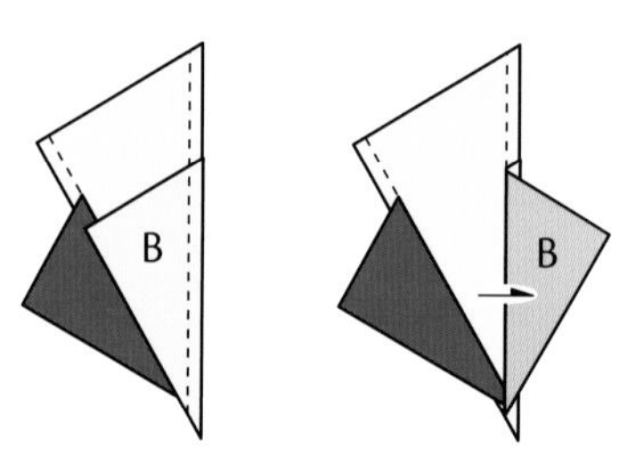

4. Use the Thirtysomething Square Up tool to trim the Thirtysomething units to 3½" x 3½". Align the inner set of angled lines marked 3" with the seams of each unit and trim the cream triangle and any excess fabric adjacent to it. Or, use a square acrylic quilter's ruler to square up each unit to 3½". The 1⅜" mark on the ruler should meet the seam lines at the edges of the 3½" unit. Trim the excess seam allowances ¼" past where the three points meet.

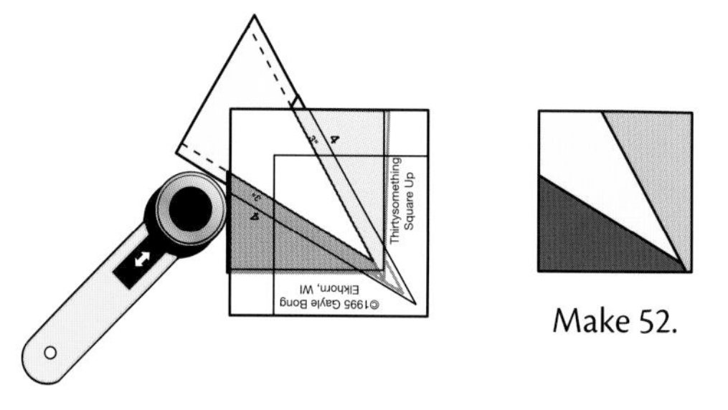
Make 52.

5. Sew together four units from step 3 to make a Thirtysomething Star block. The seams do not oppose each other as pressed, so the pieces can be sewn with the seam allowances stacked on top of each other, or you can "twist" one of them so they do oppose. Make 13 blocks.

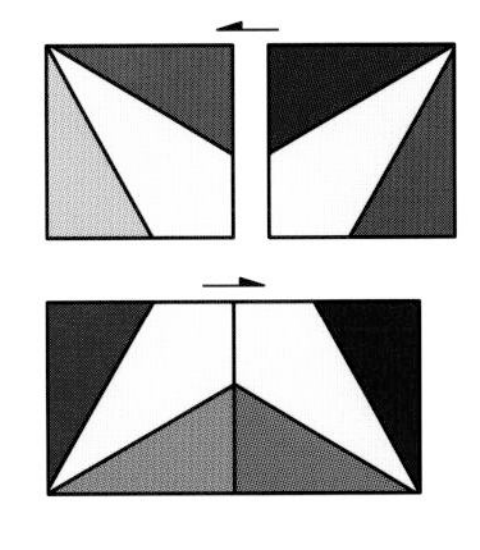
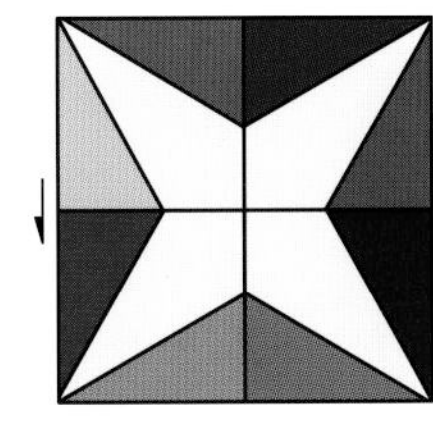

Thirtysomething Star block.
Make 13.

Making the Square-in-a-Square Blocks

Sew two medium or dark 3⅞" triangles to opposite sides of a cream square; press. Repeat with the remaining two sides. Make 12 blocks.

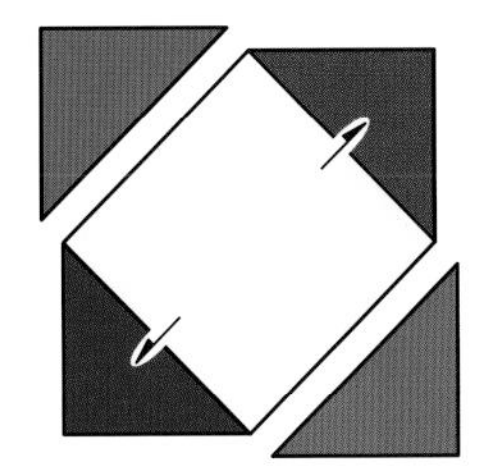
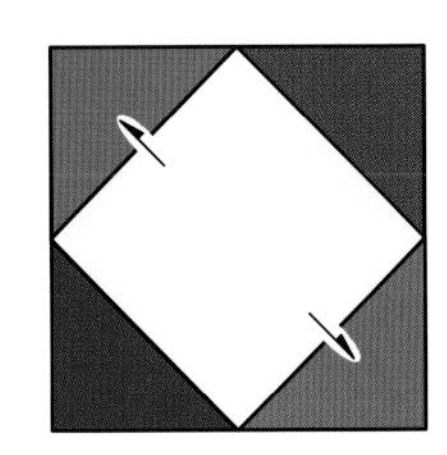

Square-in-a-Square block.
Make 12.

Making the Border Blocks

1. With pairs of medium and dark 3½" x 5" rectangles wrong sides together, place the 60° angle of your ruler along the bottom edge of the pair and trim off a triangle with 30°, 60°, and 90° corners to make 20 trapezoids and 20 reverse trapezoids. Discard the trimmed triangle.

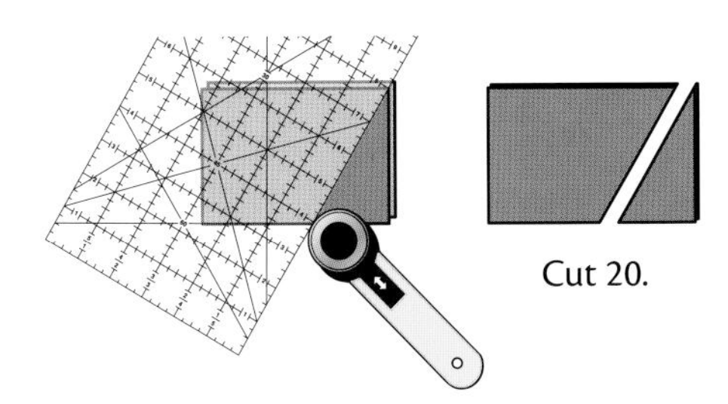

Cut 20.

2. Place the 60° line of your ruler on the long edge of a cream 3¾" x 42" strip and make the first cut near the lower-left corner of the strip to establish the angle. Rotate the ruler and place the 60° line of your ruler on the first angled cut to cut an equilateral triangle. Repeat the process, alternating the ruler between these positions to cut a total of 40 equilateral triangles.

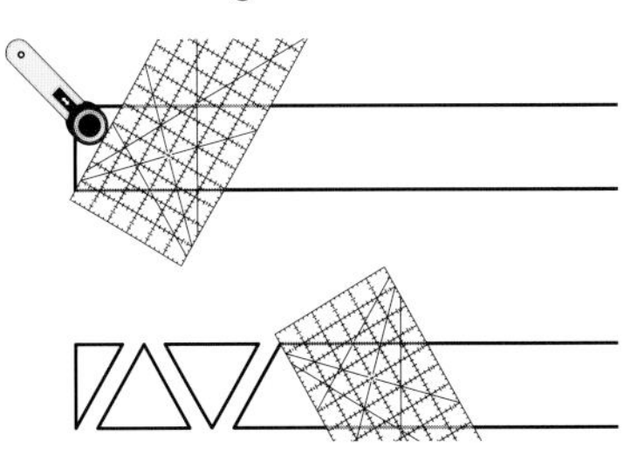

Cut 40 cream equilateral triangles.

3. Sew a cream equilateral triangle between a trapezoid and an A or B triangle as shown. To align the pieces correctly, match the 60° corner of each piece. Make 20 with the A triangle on the right and 20 with the B triangle on left.

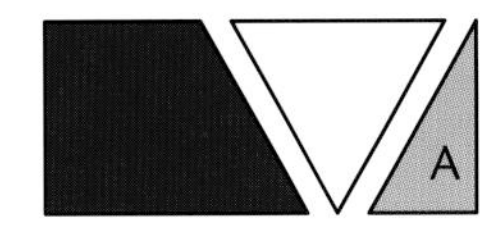

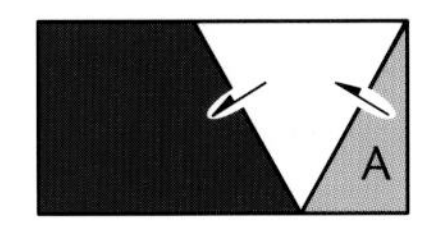

Make 20.

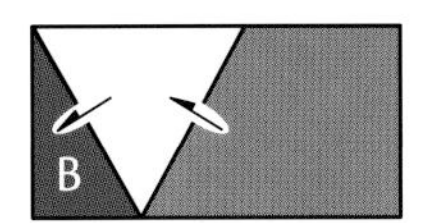

Make 20.

4. Trim each trapezoid unit to 3½" x 6½", cutting any excess from the A or B triangles.

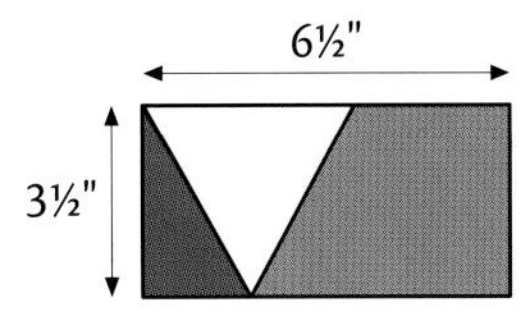

5. Sew a trapezoid unit with an A triangle to a trapezoid with a B triangle. Make 20 border blocks.

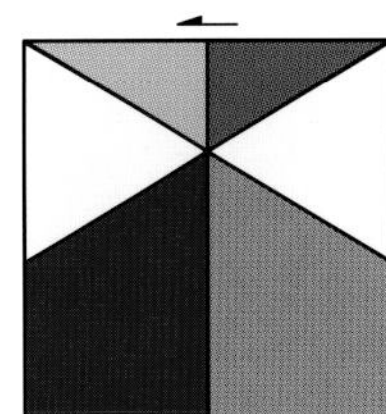

Make 20.

Making the Corner Blocks

Referring to steps 2 and 3 of "Making the Thirtysomething Star Blocks," sew a cream corner triangle between two medium or dark 4¼" x 7¼" triangles as shown to make a large Thirtysomething unit. Square up the unit to 6½". Make four corner blocks.

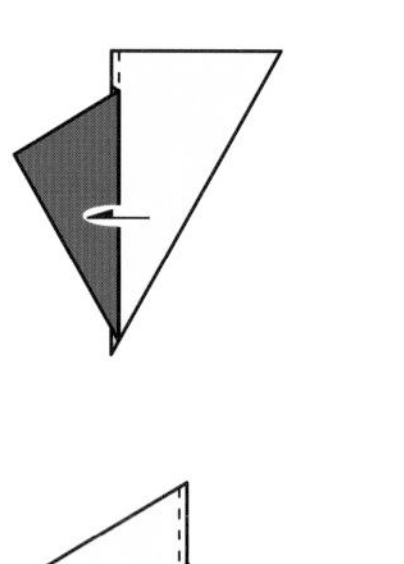

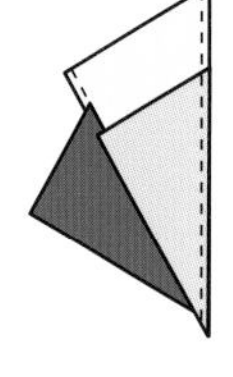

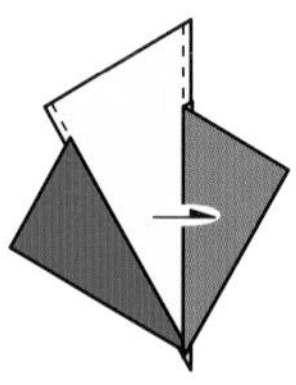

Make 4.

Assembling the Quilt Top

1. Refer to the quilt assembly diagram to arrange the Thirtysomething blocks and Square-in-a-Square blocks in five rows of five blocks each, alternating the blocks as shown. Arrange the border blocks and corner blocks around the quilt center. Sew the blocks into rows, and then sew the rows together.

Quilt assembly

2. Stay stitch ⅛" from the edge of the quilt. This will prevent the seams in the border blocks from coming loose around the edge of the quilt.

Finishing the Quilt

Refer to "Finishing Techniques" on page 16 for detailed instructions.

1. Layer the quilt top with the batting and backing; baste.
2. Hand or machine quilt. Follow the quilting suggestions shown below or use your own design.

Quilting diagram

3. Use the 2¼"-wide strips to bind the edges of your quilt.

Maggie's **Star**

Pieced and quilted by Gayle Bong

Two simple stars combine to make this new block. This pretty palette was developed from sorting all my fat quarters by color. Add two light background fabrics for interest, and you have the start of a great quilt recipe. You could use one fat quarter both as the outer star and as an inner accent in another star as long as there's contrast.

Finished quilt: 51½" x 63½"

Finished block: 12"

Materials

Yardages are based on 42"-wide fabric.

12 fat quarters of assorted prints for blocks and borders

2 yards of cream fabric 1 for block and border backgrounds

⅞ yard of cream fabric 2 for block backgrounds

½ yard *total* of assorted accent fabrics for block centers

½ yard of fabric for binding

3⅝ yards of fabric for backing

58" x 70" piece of batting

Cutting		
Please read all the instructions before starting.		
FABRIC	FIRST CUT	FOLLOWING CUT(S)
Assorted prints	1 strip each, 2½" x 20" (12 total)	4 rectangles, 2½" x 4¼" (48 total)
	2 strips each, 3⅞" x 20"* (24 total)	7 squares, 3⅞" x 3⅞"; cut each square in half diagonally to make 14 triangles (168 total; you will use 160)
	1 strip each, 2" x 20" (12 total)	
Assorted accents	12 rectangles, 3½" x 12"	2 rectangles, 3½" x 6"; cut each rectangle in half diagonally to make 4 C triangles (48 total)
Cream 1	3 strips, 3½" x 42"	28 squares, 3½" x 3½"
	2 strips, 7¼" x 42"	6 squares, 7¼" x 7¼"; cut each square into quarters diagonally to make 24 triangles
	4 strips, 3⅞" x 42"	32 squares, 3⅞" x 3⅞"; cut each square in half diagonally to make 64 triangles
	11 strips, 2" x 42"	
Cream 2	3 strips, 3½" x 42"	24 squares, 3½" x 3½"
	2 strips, 7¼" x 42"	6 squares, 7¼" x 7¼"; cut each square into quarters diagonally to make 24 triangles
Binding fabric	6 strips, 2¼" x 42"	
**Refer to "Cutting Triangles Using a Triangle-Cutting Ruler" on page 13 for an alternate way to cut triangles from 3½" strips.*		

Making the Blocks

Keep matching fabrics together so one fat quarter, one accent fabric, and one cream fabric are used in each block. After sewing each seam, press the seam allowances in the direction indicated by the arrows.

1. Place pairs of matching 2½" x 4¼" rectangles wrong sides together. Cut the rectangles diagonally to make 4 matching A triangles and 4 matching B triangles for each block (48 total A triangles and 48 total B triangles). Separate the A triangles from the B triangles and label each stack.

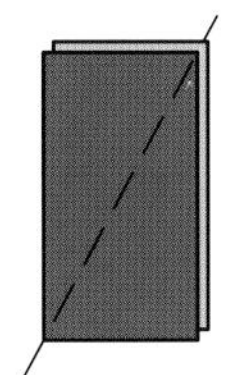

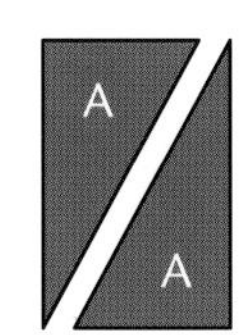

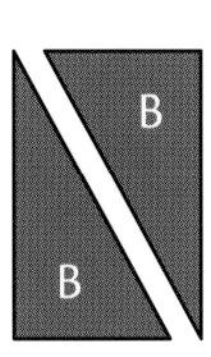

Cut 4 A and 4 B triangles
(48 of each, 96 total).

2. Match the points of an A triangle with a C triangle. Start stitching the triangles together at the broad end of the accent triangle. The smaller A triangle will be underneath. Hold the point straight while pressing the seam allowances toward the A triangle. Press carefully to avoid tucks, particularly at the point. Do not trim the point until after the next step. Make four units.

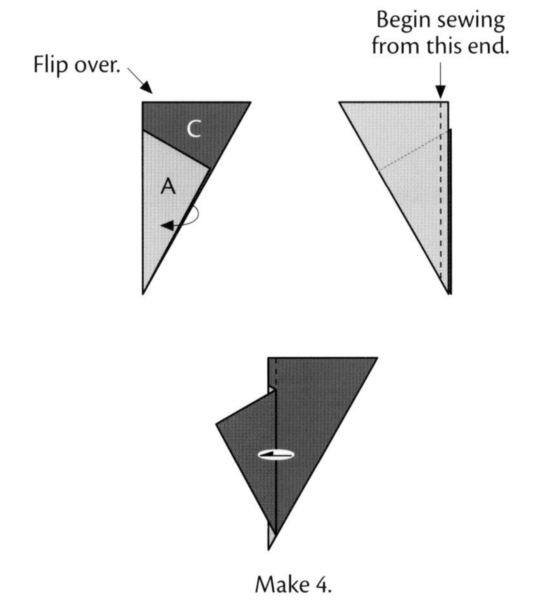

Make 4.

Points to Remember

Be sure to sew on the long bias edge of the A and B triangles. The broad end of the C triangle may point in one direction, and then the other. Ignore this as you sew; the excess fabric will be trimmed off later.

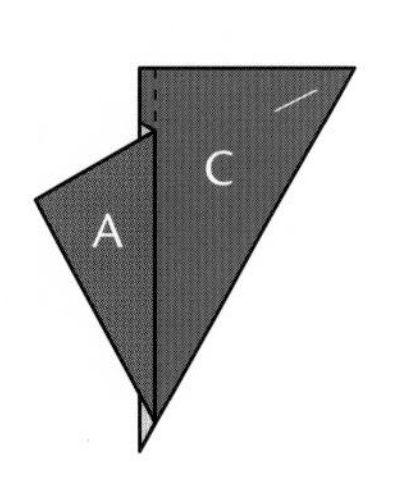

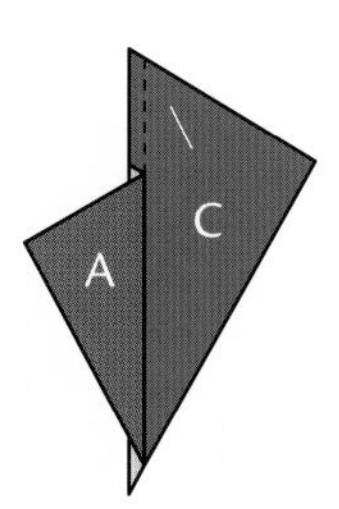

3. Place a B triangle right sides together with the C triangle of a unit from step 3, aligning the raw edges of the three narrow points. Start stitching at the broad end of the C triangle. Press the seam allowances toward the B triangle. Make four Thirtysomething units.

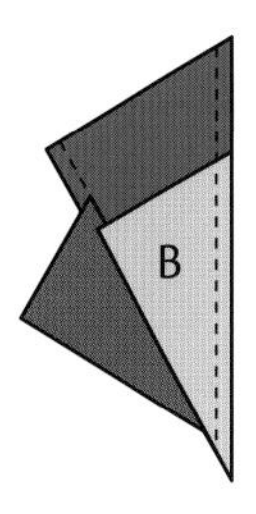

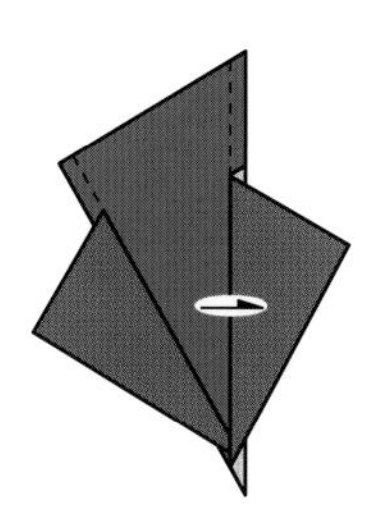

4. Use the Thirtysomething Square Up tool to trim the Thirtysomething units to 3½" x 3½". Align the inner set of angled lines marked 3" with the seams of the unit and trim the accent triangle and any excess fabric adjacent to it. Or, use a square acrylic quilter's ruler to square up the units to 3½". The 1⅜" mark on the ruler should meet the seam lines at the edges of the 3½" unit. Trim the excess seam allowances ¼" past where the three points meet.

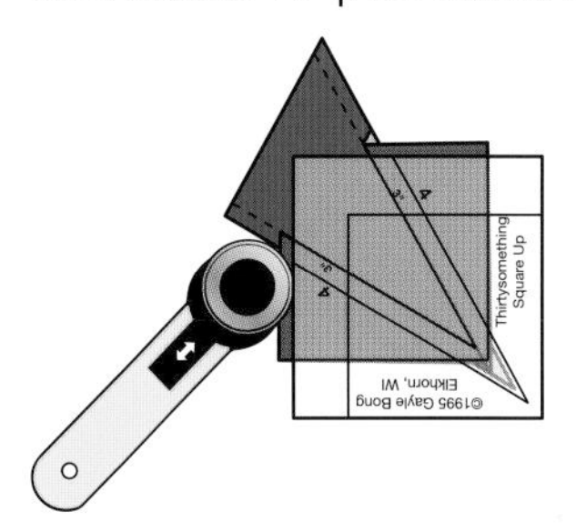

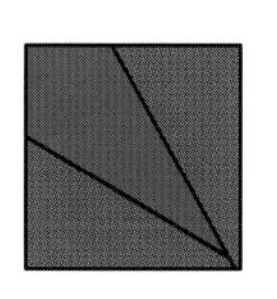

Make 4.

5. Sew together four Thirtysomething units to make a Thirtysomething star unit. The seams do not oppose each other as pressed, so the pieces can be sewn with the seam allowances stacked on top of each other, or you can "twist" one of them so they do oppose.

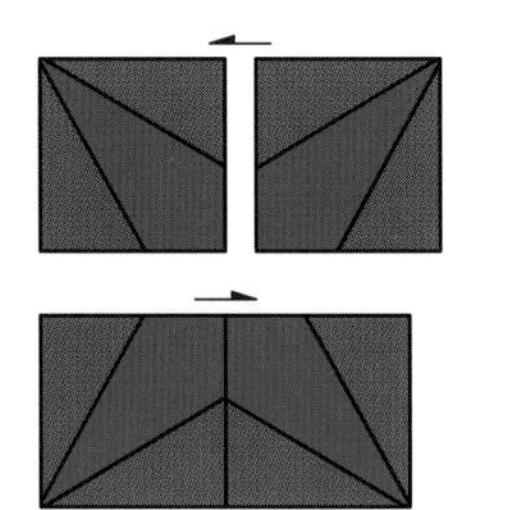
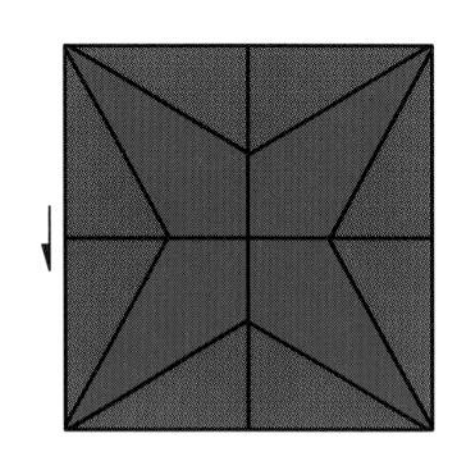

6. Sew 3⅞" triangles to adjacent short edges of a cream 7¼" triangle. Make four flying-geese units.

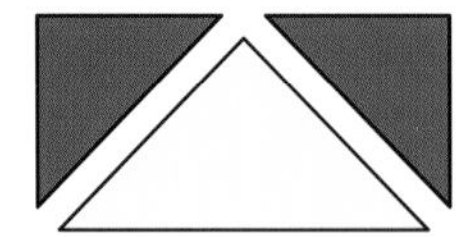
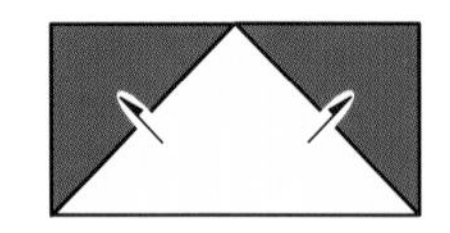

Make 4.

7. Arrange four cream squares, four flying-geese units, and the Thirtysomething star unit. Sew the units into rows, and then sew the rows together.

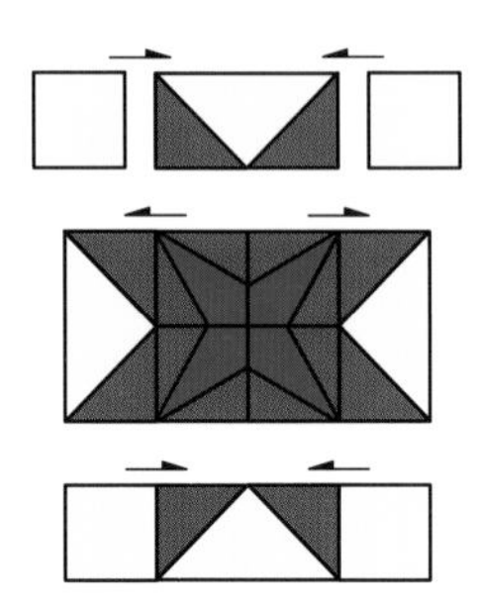
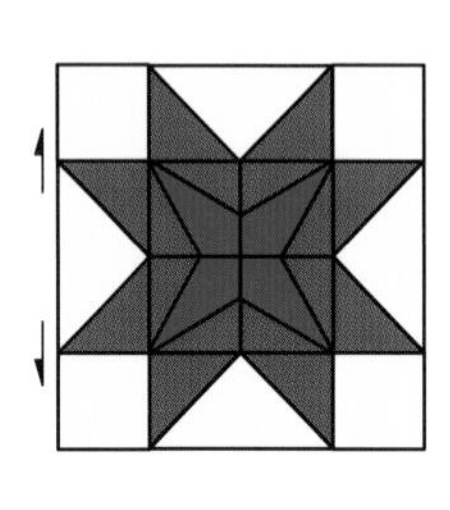

8. Repeat steps 2–8 to make a total of 12 blocks, six with cream 1 background pieces and six with cream 2 background pieces.

Assembling the Quilt Top

1. Refer to the quilt assembly diagram on page 83 to sew the blocks into four rows of three blocks each, alternating backgrounds. Sew the rows together.
2. Attach cream 2"-wide strips to the quilt top, referring to "Adding Borders" on page 15 to measure, cut, and sew them.
3. Cut the fat quarter 2"-wide strips into various lengths, and then randomly sew them together end to end to make one long strip. The shorter you cut the strips the more variety you'll have in each border. Attach the borders to the quilt top.

4. Sew a cream triangle to a fat quarter triangle to make a half-square-triangle unit. Make 64 units.

Make 64.

5. Sew 18 half-square-triangle units together as shown to make the side borders. Repeat to make a total of two border strips. Stitch the borders to the sides of the quilt top. Sew 14 half-square-triangle units together as shown to make the top border. Add a cream 1 square to each end of the strip. Repeat to make the bottom border. Stitch the strips to the top and bottom edges of the quilt top.

Side border.
Make 2.

Top/bottom border.
Make 2.

6. Attach cream 2"-wide strips to the quilt top.

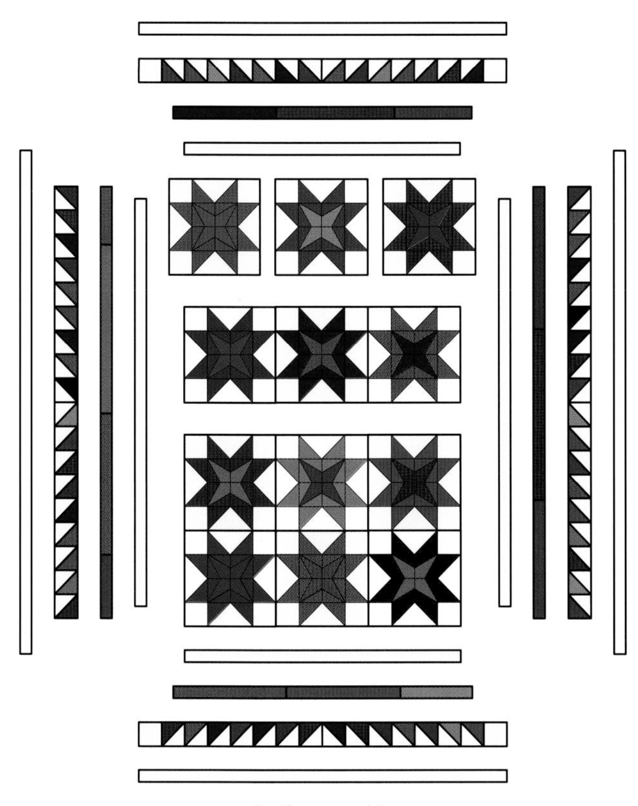

Quilt assembly

Finishing the Quilt

Refer to "Finishing Techniques" on page 16 for detailed instructions.

1. Layer the quilt top with the batting and backing; baste.
2. Hand or machine quilt. Follow the quilting suggestions shown below or use your own design.

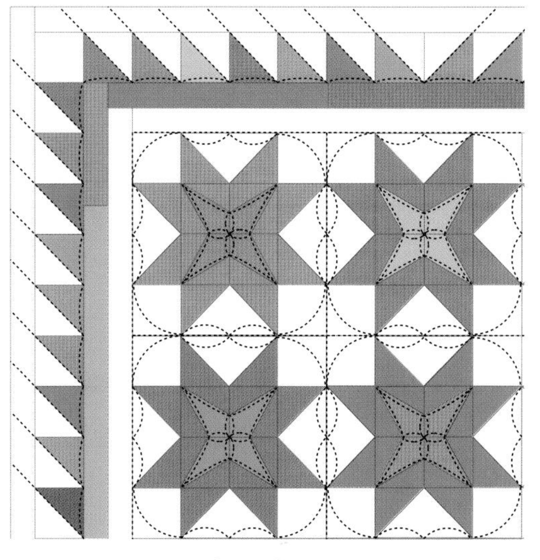

Quilting diagram

3. Use the 2¼"-wide strips to bind the edges of your quilt.

Vintage **LeMoyne** Stars

Pieced and quilted by Gayle Bong

The classic LeMoyne Star made with reproduction 1800s prints is perfect for me. The LeMoyne Star looks great no matter what fabric is chosen. Search your scraps for prints with the same character. Instead of starting with the fat quarters and making more scraps, start with your smaller scraps first. The diamonds in the stars are cut from 2¼"-wide strips, but a 2½"-wide strip could always be trimmed down.

Finished quilt: 60" x 77"

Finished block: 8½"

Materials

Yardages are based on 42"-wide fabric.

2⅛ yards *total* of assorted dark scraps for blocks and borders

1⅞ yards *total* of assorted light scraps for blocks and borders

1 yard *total* of assorted medium scraps for blocks and borders

⅞ yard of cream fabric for inner-border background

⅝ yard of fabric for binding

4⅛ yards of fabric for backing

64" x 80" piece of batting

Cutting

Please read all the instructions before starting.

FABRIC	FIRST CUT	FOLLOWING CUT(S)
For each light LeMoyne Star border block (cut 28 sets of pieces; keep pieces for each set together)		
Assorted light scraps	1 strip, 2¼" x 18" (28 total)	4 diamonds* (112 total)
Assorted medium scraps	1 strip, 2¼" x 18" (28 total)	4 diamonds* (112 total)
Assorted dark scraps	1 strip, 4¾" x 18" (28 total)	1 square, 4¾" x 4¾"; cut the square into quarters diagonally to make 4 triangles (112 total). Trim the remainder of the strip to 3" wide and cut 4 squares, 3" x 3" (112 total).
For each dark LeMoyne Star block (cut 24 sets of pieces; keep pieces for each set together)		
Assorted light scraps	1 strip, 4¾" x 18" (24 total)	1 square, 4¾" x 4¾"; cut the square into quarters diagonally to make 4 triangles (96 total). Trim the remainder of the strip to 3" wide and cut 4 squares, 3" x 3" (96 total).
Assorted medium scraps	1 strip, 2¼" x 18" (24 total)	4 diamonds* (96 total)
Assorted dark scraps	1 strip, 2¼" x 18" (24 total)	4 diamonds* (96 total)
For inner border and binding		
Cream	4 squares, 4⅝" x 4⅝"	
	4 strips, 5" x 42"	30 squares, 5" x 5"; cut each square in half diagonally to make 60 triangles**
Assorted dark scraps	30 squares, 3⅝" x 3⅝"	Cut each square in half diagonally to make 60 triangles
Binding fabric	7 strips, 2¼" x 42"	

**To cut diamonds from 2¼" strip, align the 45° line of your ruler on a long edge of your strip of fabric and cut to establish the angle. Make four more cuts at the same angle, 2¼" apart.*

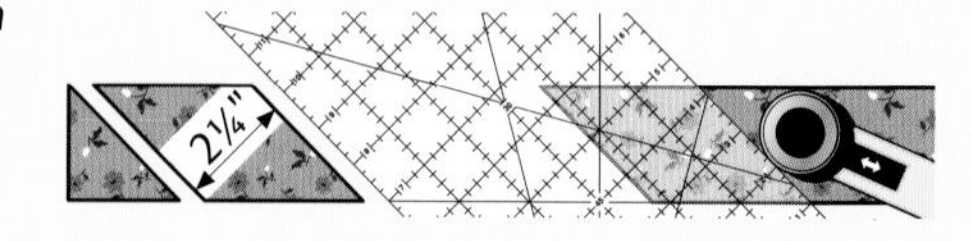

***With pairs of triangles wrong sides together, trim the top point of the triangles to leave trapezoids 3¼" tall.*

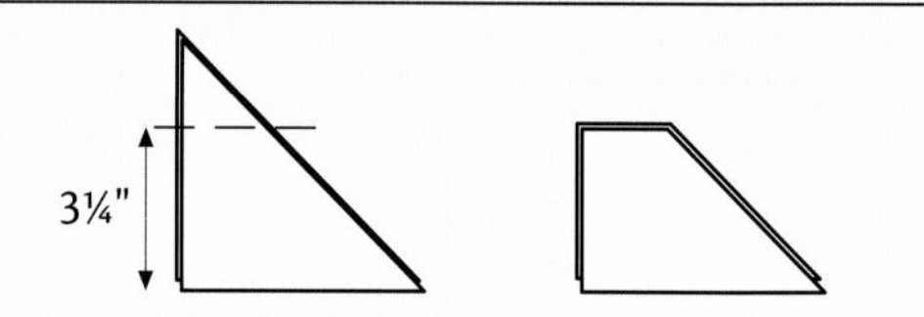

Making the Light LeMoyne Star Blocks

After sewing each seam, press the seam allowances in the direction indicated by the arrows.

1. Choose one set of light LeMoyne Star block pieces. With the light diamond on top, sew each light diamond to a medium diamond. Avoid stitching into the seam allowance at the inside corners indicated by the dot in the illustration. Make 4.

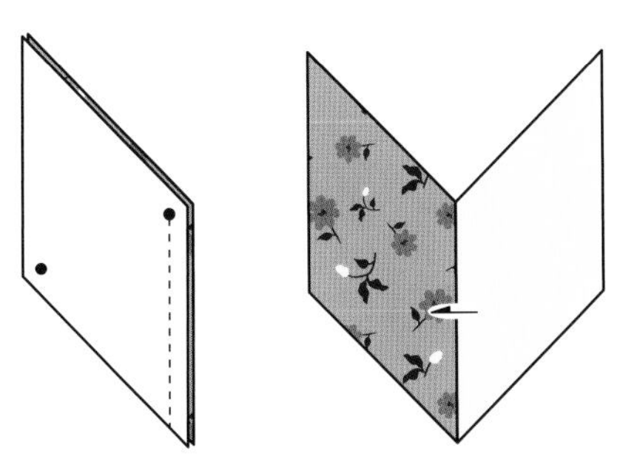

2. In the same manner, sew two pairs of diamonds together to make a half-star unit, and then sew the two half-star units together. Before pressing, undo two stitches in the seam allowance at the center of the star. This will let the seam allowances fall open in a pinwheel fashion, which will help distribute the bulk at the center of the block. Be careful not to stretch the bias edge of the diamonds as you press.

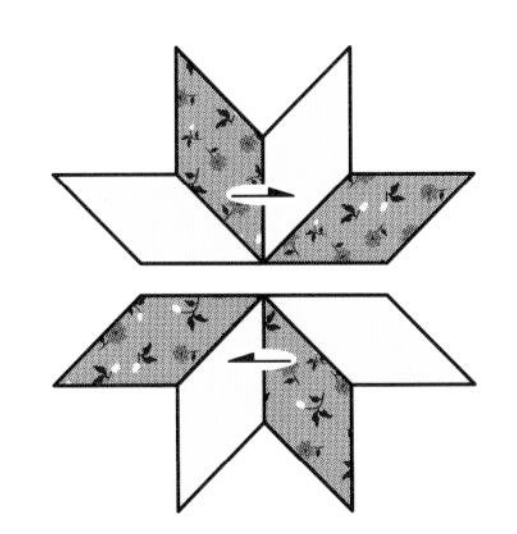

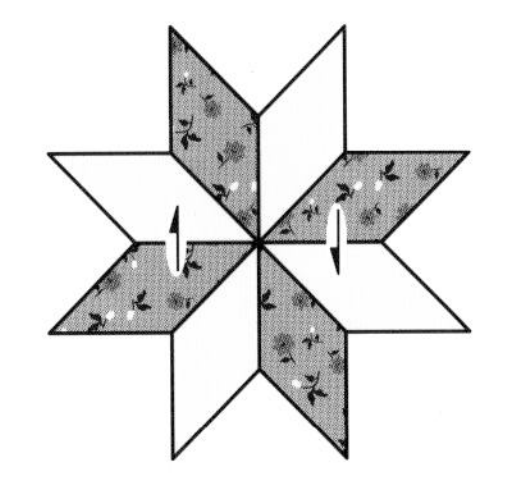

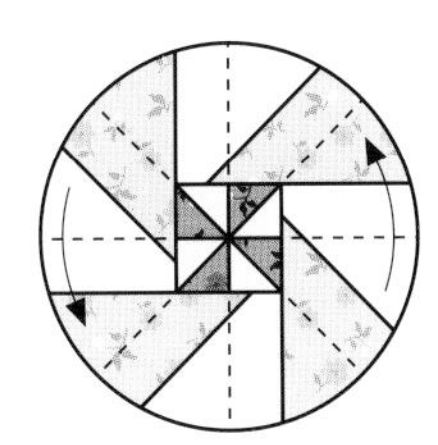

How to Sew Set-In Pieces

The seams of typical patchwork run from raw edge to raw edge, crossing into the seam allowances at each end. There are many beautiful patterns that require set-in seams where stitching stops at an inside corner where three seams meet. It takes just a little practice on a few blocks to master them. To aid in accomplishing this, I find it most helpful to use an open-toe presser foot, so it's easier to see exactly where I'm sewing.

It helps to mark the seam intersections on the back of each patch with a dot, and then match the dots as you sew. A template to mark the seam allowances is helpful. Poke a hole in the template where the seams intersect using a large needle. Align the edges of the template with the edges of the patch and make a mark using a pencil through the hole. An alternate method is to mark the back of each patch with an X where the seams intersect. Measure ¼" from each edge of the patch and make a mark. Even if you visualize the dot, it helps to use a pin to indicate precisely where the seam begins or ends at the inside corner; then the seams may be sewn from either direction.

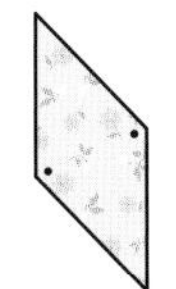

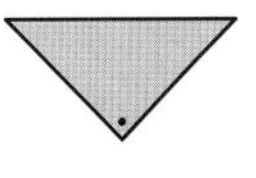

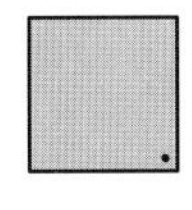

Backstitching is required where the three seams meet because there will not be seams crossing one another to anchor the threads. Some machines seem to be a little fussy about responding to the backstitch lever, so I suggest backstitching four to five stitches away from the intersection. This way if any stitches do cross into the seam allowance, they can be removed without cutting backstitches.

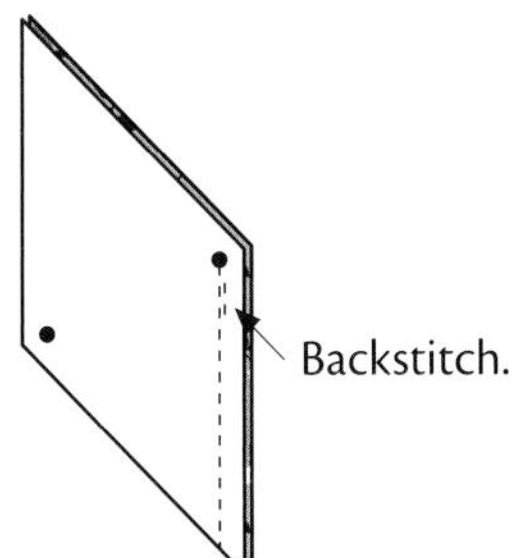

3. Sew dark triangles between the star points at the sides of the block. With right sides together, match points of a medium diamond and a dark triangle as shown. Stitch the seam, clip the threads, and remove the pieces from the machine. Match the other point of the dark triangle to the light diamond and sew. Press the seam allowances of the set-in background pieces to pinwheel as described in step 2. Repeat with all four triangles.

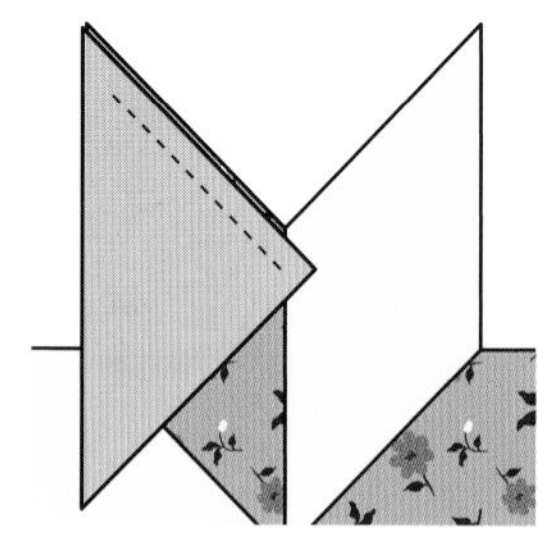

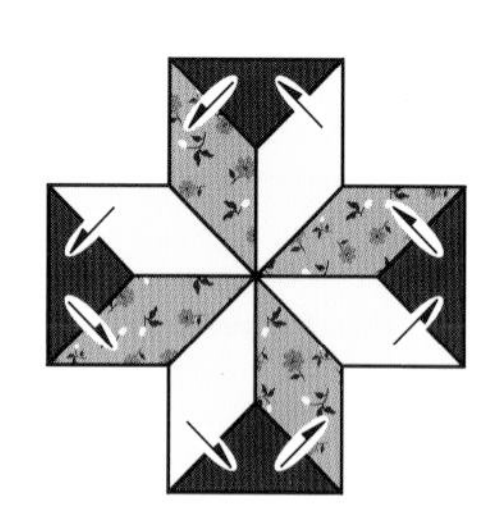

4. Sew a dark square into each corner in the same manner. Press the seam allowances of the set-in background pieces to pinwheel as described in step 2.

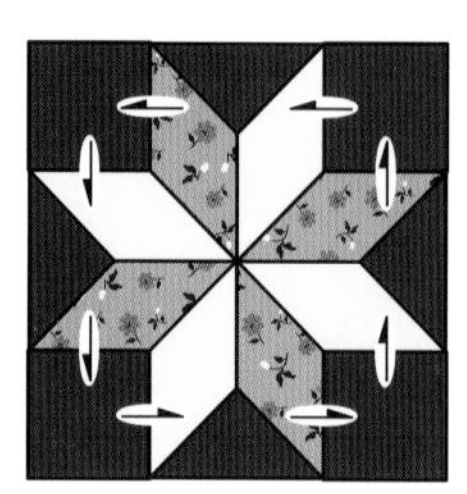

Light Star block.
Make 28.

5. Repeat steps 1–4 to make a total of 28 light LeMoyne Star blocks.

Making the Dark LeMoyne Star Blocks

Choose one set of dark Star pieces. Refer to "Making the Light LeMoyne Star Block" to make 24 blocks in the same manner, sewing the diamond pairs together with the medium diamond on top and using the light background pieces.

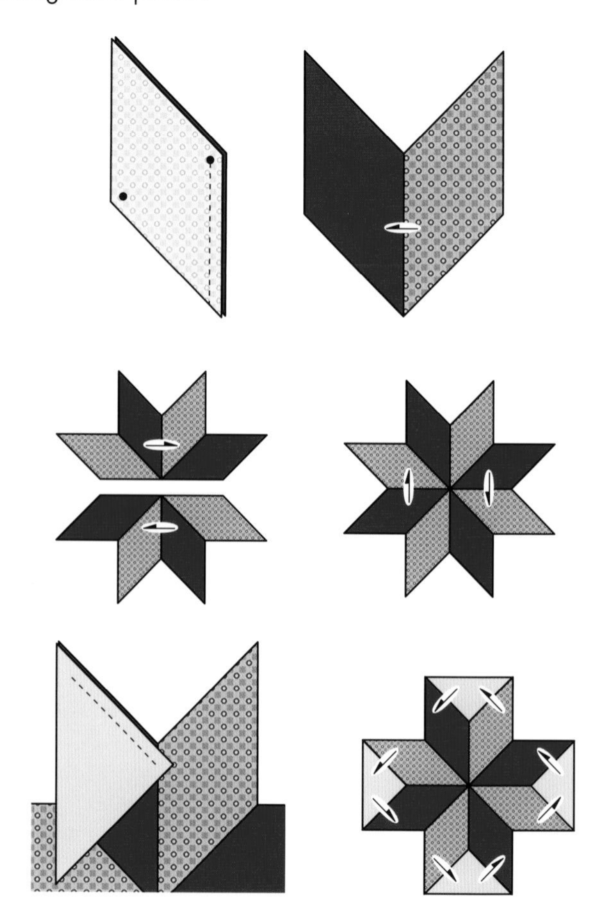

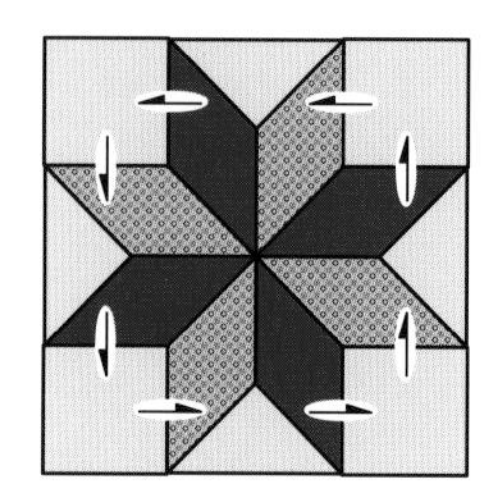

Dark LeMoyne Star block.
Make 24.

Assembling the Quilt Top

1. Arrange the dark LeMoyne Star blocks in six rows of four blocks each. When you're happy with the color arrangement, sew the blocks into rows, and then sew the rows together.
2. Sew a dark triangle to the angled edge of each cream trapezoid. Make 30 units with the triangle on the right side and 30 units with the triangle on the left side.

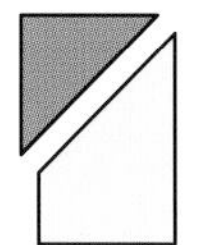

Make 30 each.

3. Join 12 trapezoid units as shown. Repeat to make a total of two border strips. Add a cream square to the ends of each strip to make the top and bottom borders. Join 18 trapezoid units as shown. Repeat to make a total of two side border strips.

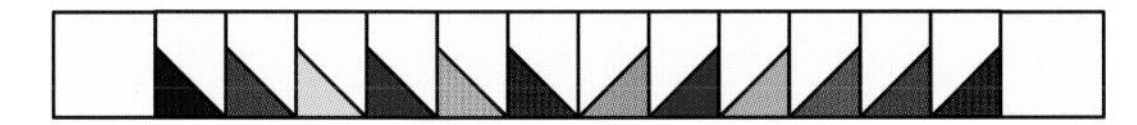

Top/bottom border.
Make 2.

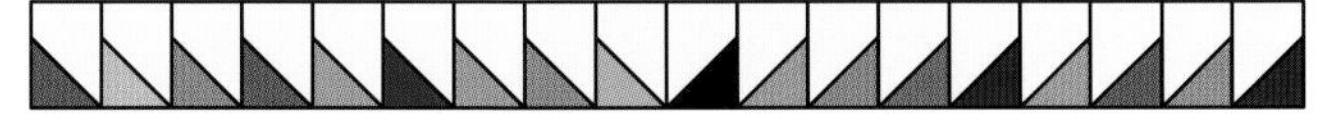

Side border.
Make 2.

4. Sew the side borders to the sides of the quilt top, matching the seam of every third unit to the seams between the blocks. Ease to fit as necessary. Sew the top and bottom borders to the top and bottom edges of the quilt top.
5. Arrange the light LeMoyne Star blocks around the quilt center until you're happy with the color arrangement. Sew the seven blocks along each side together, and then stitch the strips to the sides of the quilt top. Sew the blocks along the top and bottom together, and then stitch the strips to the top and bottom edges of the quilt top.

Quilt assembly

6. Stay stitch 1⁄8" from the edge of the quilt. This will prevent the seams in the blocks from coming loose around the edges of the quilt.

Finishing the Quilt

Refer to "Finishing Techniques" on page 16 for detailed instructions.

1. Layer the quilt top with the batting and backing; baste.
2. Hand or machine quilt. Follow the quilting suggestions shown below or use your own design.

Quilting diagram

3. Use the 2¼"-wide strips to bind the edges of your quilt.

Leap Year

Pieced and quilted by Gayle Bong

I fell in love with the Log Cabin block when I made this quilt. I'd only ever made a few blocks before, but I already know I'll be making more Log Cabin quilts. I chose 16 fat quarters and used each print in four blocks. To use smaller scraps, cut the "logs" for one block from one strip, 1½" x 30", or for two blocks from three strips, 1½" x 21". Cut the larger pieces first with this project. That way the smallest pieces can be cut from the ends of the strips that the big pieces were cut from.

Finished quilt: 64½" x 64½"

Finished block: 7"

Materials

Yardages are based on 42"-wide fabric.

3 yards of black fabric for blocks, inner and outer borders, and binding

16 fat quarters of assorted bright batiks for blocks

⅜ yard of red fabric for block centers

⅓ yard of multicolored batik for middle border

4 yards of fabric for backing

68" x 68" piece of batting

Cutting

Please read all the instructions before starting.

FABRIC	FIRST CUT	FOLLOWING CUT
Red	4 strips, 2½" x 42"	64 squares, 2½" x 2½"
Assorted bright batiks	6 strips from each, 1½" x 21" (96 total)	4 logs, 1½" x 7½" (64 total)
		4 logs, 1½" x 6½" (64 total)
		4 logs, 1½" x 5½" (64 total)
		4 logs, 1½" x 4½" (64 total)
		4 logs, 1½" x 3½" (64 total)
		4 logs, 1½" x 2½" (64 total)
Black	33 strips, 1½" x 42"	64 logs, 1½" x 6½"
		64 logs, 1½" x 5½"
		64 logs, 1½" x 4½"
		64 logs, 1½" x 3½"
	6 strips, 1½" x 42"	
	6 strips, 2½" x 42"	
	4 squares, 4½" x 4½"	
	7 strips, 2¼" x 42"	
Multicolored batik	6 strips, 1½" x 42"	

Making the Blocks

Use matching batik logs for each block. The red center square will be off center in the finished block. Press the seam allowances away from the center square after each piece is added.

1. Sew a batik 1½" x 2½" log to a red square; press.

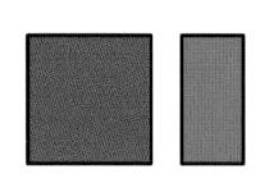
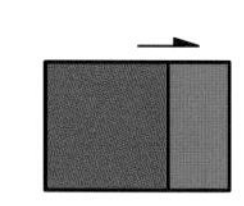

Make 64.

2. Rotate the unit so the batik log is at the top and right side up. Sew a batik 1½" x 3½" log to the right edge; press.

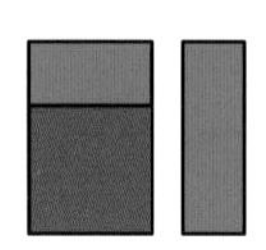
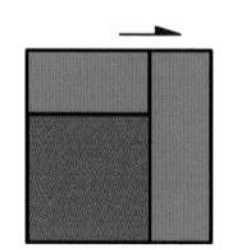

Make 64.

3. Rotate the unit so the newly added log is at the top. Sew a black 1½" x 3½" log to the right edge; press.

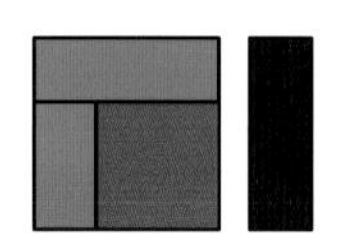
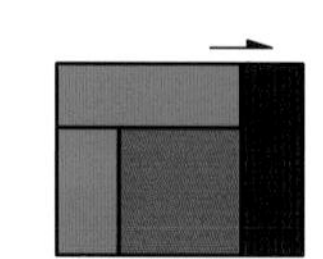

4. Rotate the unit so the newly added log is at the top. Sew a black 1½" x 4½" log to the right edge; press.

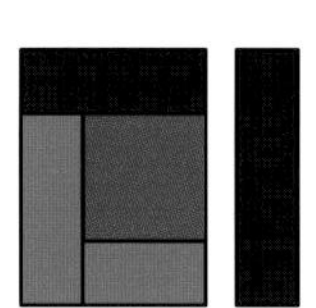
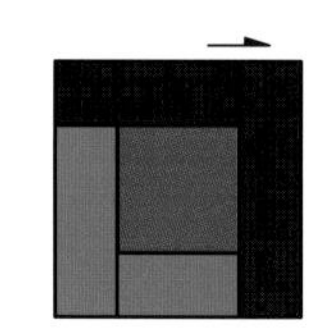

5. Rotate the unit so the newly added log is at the top. Continue adding matching batik logs and black logs in the positions shown.

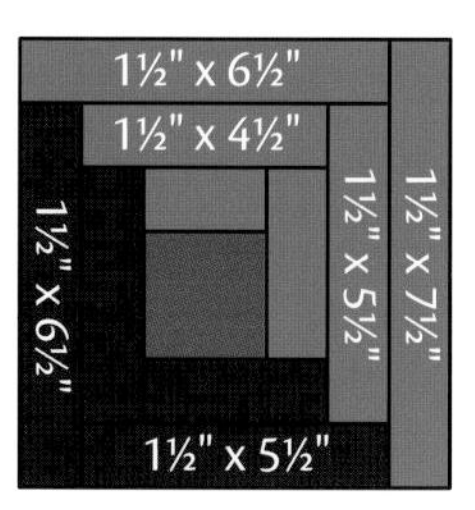

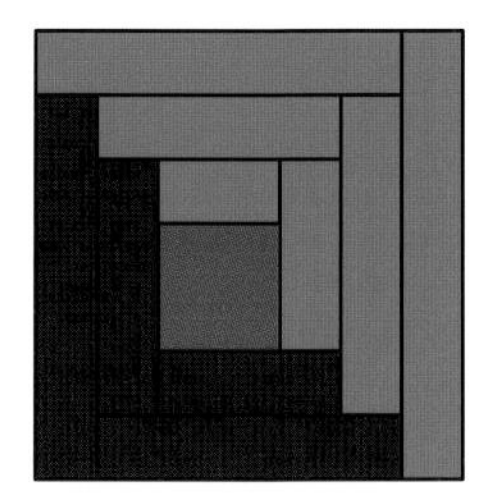

Make 64.

6. Repeat steps 1–5 to make a total of 64 blocks.

Quick Placement Check

Starting with the fourth log (the second black log), the logs are always added to the side that has two seams to cross.

Assembling the Quilt Top

1. Arrange the blocks in eight rows of eight blocks each as shown or as desired; there are many arrangements possible using the Log Cabin block and you might find a setting you like more. Sew the blocks into rows, and then sew the rows together; press.
2. Sew the black 1½"-wide strips together end to end. Repeat with the multicolored batik 1½"-wide strips and the black 2½"-wide strips. Sew the batik strip to the black 1½"-wide strip along the long edges; press the seam allowances toward

the black fabric. Sew the black 2½"-wide strip to the opposite long edge of the batik strip. Press the seam allowances toward the black strip. Referring to "Adding Borders" on page 15, measure and cut four borders from the border strip set. Attach two borders to opposite sides of the quilt top. Sew a black 4½" square to each end of the remaining two borders and sew them to the quilt top and bottom edges.

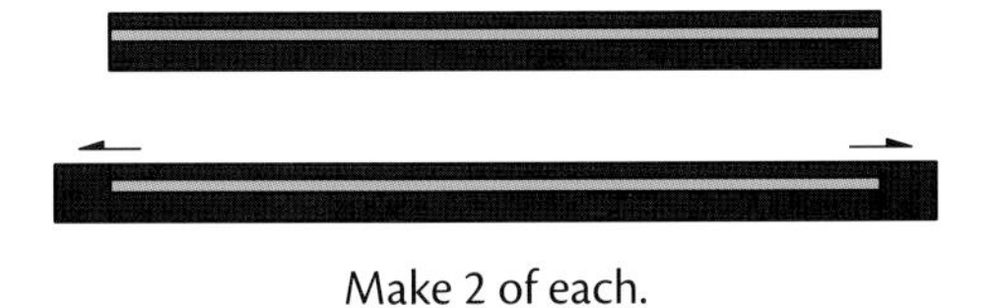

Make 2 of each.

Quilt assembly

Finishing the Quilt

Refer to "Finishing Techniques" on page 16 for detailed instructions.

1. Layer the quilt top with the batting and backing; baste.
2. Hand or machine quilt. Follow the quilting suggestions shown below or use your own design.

Quilting diagram

3. Use the black 2¼"-wide strips to bind the edges of your quilt.

About the **Author**

Gayle Bong has been an avid quiltmaker for 27 years. She first learned to sew by watching her mother, and by ninth grade she was making most of her own clothes. Designing quilts and writing patterns come naturally to Gayle, who has always been attracted to geometric patterns, fabric, math, puzzles, and writing. She's particularly passionate about her fast, contemporary cutting and piecing techniques and shares them enthusiastically in her classes. In her spare time she enjoys reading, hiking, gardening, and helping her friends and neighbors wherever needed. This is Gayle's eighth book on quiltmaking.

There's More Online!

Read about Gayle's latest quilting adventures on her blog, http://gaylebong.blogspot.com.

Find more great quilt books at www.martingale-pub.com.

You might also enjoy these other fine titles from **Martingale & Company**

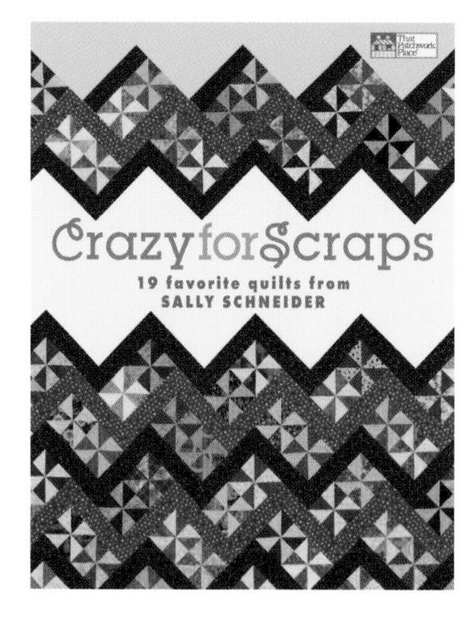

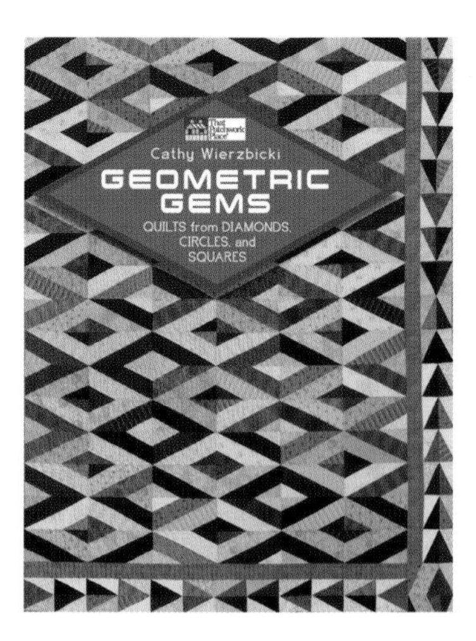

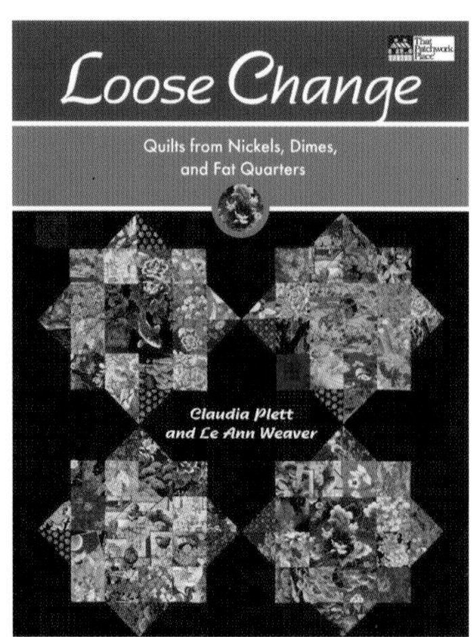

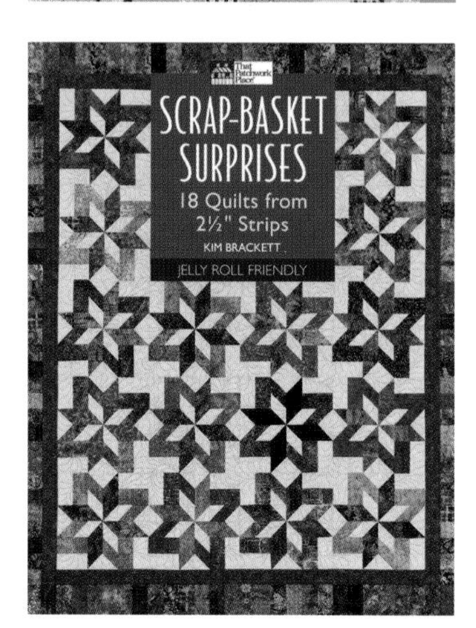

Our books are available at bookstores and your favorite craft, fabric, and yarn retailers.
Visit us at www.martingale-pub.com or contact us at:

1-800-426-3126
International: 1-425-483-3313
Fax: 1-425-486-7596
Email: info@martingale-pub.com